THE LOST SECRET

THE LOST SECRET

Unlocking the Hidden Chapters of
Napoleon Hill's

THINK AND GROW RICH

MONICA MAIN

Waterside Productions
Cardiff-by-the-Sea, California

With appreciation to the Napoleon Hill Foundation for permission to quote extracts from *Think and Grow Rich*. All material from the book is presented verbatim, with the original spelling, grammar, and punctuation.

Printed in the United States of America

First Printing, 2019

ISBN-13: 978-1-941768-16-7 (print edition)
ISBN-13: 978-1-941768-17-4 (ebook edition)
ISBN-13: 978-1-941768-18-1 (audio edition)

Waterside Productions
2055 Oxford Avenue
Cardiff-by-the-Sea, CA 92007
www.waterside.com

DEDICATED TO
NAPOLEON HILL

*With gratitude for his continuing inspiration to
write this book and to help carry the torch of his
original work, created almost a century ago*

CONTENTS

Foreword by Jack Canfield ix

Preface xi

Introduction: The Mystery Behind How This Secret
Came to the Surface xv

Chapter 1: Can Anyone Really "Think and Grow Rich"? 1

Chapter 2: The First Step Toward Riches:
What Is Your Burning Desire? 9

Chapter 3: The Second Step Toward Riches:
Unwavering Faith Through Just "Knowing" 25

Chapter 4: The Third Step Toward Riches:
Auto-Suggestion, Visualization, and Affirmations 47

Chapter 5: The Fourth Step Toward Riches:
Specialized Knowledge for Big Bucks 63

Chapter 6: The Fifth Step Toward Riches:
It's in Your Imagination 77

Chapter 7: The Sixth Step Toward Riches:
Creating Your Grand Plan 95

Chapter 8: The Seventh Step Toward Riches:
The Power of Decision 105

Chapter 9: The Eighth Step Toward Riches:
Persistence and Your Force of Will..115

Chapter 10: The Ninth Step Toward Riches:
Bringing Forth Your Personal Power..125

Chapter 11: The Tenth Step Toward Riches:
How to Use Sex Transmutation to Attain Your Deepest Desires 137

Chapter 12: The Eleventh Step Toward Riches:
Getting Your Subconscious Mind to Work for You 143

Chapter 13: The Twelfth Step Toward Riches:
How the Brain Receives Ideas and Inspiration 151

Chapter 14: The Thirteenth Step Toward Riches:
How to Use the Power of the Sixth Sense..157

Chapter 15: The Fourteenth Step Toward Riches:
Moving Beyond Fear 161

Preface to the Lost Chapters..167

Lost Chapter 16: Transcending above the Common Man..................169

Lost Chapter 17: Summoning Desires Through the Ether.................179

Conclusion 189

Afterword by Bob Proctor 193

Final Thoughts from Monica Main 195

About Napoleon Hill..197

About Monica Main 199

FOREWORD

Napoleon Hill knew more about how to manifest wealth, abundance, health, and happiness than any author writing books in the twentieth century. His seminal book *Think and Grow Rich* has inspired hundreds of millions of readers over the last eighty years to pursue and achieve their dreams. Monica Main is the first author of the twenty-first century to significantly enhance Hill's teachings in such a way as to make them immediately accessible to all readers—whatever their background, previous education, or exposure to concepts such as the law of attraction or the power of masterminds.

Napoleon Hill lived at a time when there were few women in the world of business. Most females living in the United States when *Think and Grow Rich* was first published in 1937 were stay-at-home moms supporting the men in their lives, who were considered to be the "breadwinners." Hill was as progressive as any man could be in 1937, but he could not avoid the cultural bias that downplayed the role of women in economic matters. And as a result, most of *Think and Grow Rich* was written in a style that doesn't address the ability of women to manifest wealth.

In *The Lost Secret*, Monica Main has rectified this deficiency. She is a woman who became an adult in the twenty-first century, and by following the principles and practices Napoleon Hill wrote about in *Think and Grow Rich*, she is now able to write from her own experience and perspective in a way that makes Hill's original teachings more easily understood and actionable by a wider and more diverse audience.

In *The Lost Secret*, Monica pinpoints the essence of Napoleon Hill's breakthrough thinking and highlights the most important principle that Hill revealed in his speeches and writings—that of "vibration" and how a clear understanding of how to raise one's vibration is the key to manifesting wealth, health, and happiness. Monica writes about this principle of vibration in a way that I believe resonates with today's more sophisticated audience. She speculates that the two chapters Hill wrote on the importance of raising one's vibration, which have been previously lost until now, were excluded from the original 1937 publication of *Think and Grow Rich* because they would have been considered too metaphysical and too far out for the readers at that time. But today, with our greater knowledge and understanding of quantum physics and concepts such as "the zero point," we now see that Hill's insights into the power of vibration have a clear scientific basis, which Monica documents in this book.

As you read *The Lost Secret*, you will be presented with Napoleon Hill's original thinking . . . *and* you will also learn from Monica's experiences in applying Hill's principles to her own life as a woman and as a modern-day business leader. The wonderful combination of knowledge and experience she shares in this powerful book has the potential to significantly change your life forever.

And as both Napoleon Hill and Monica explain, it is by focusing on how you can best serve others that you will create your own abundance. The universe is not a zero-sum game. There is enough for everyone to live an abundant and fulfilling life. And as you will soon discover within these pages, it is now time for you, too, to unleash your hidden powers and create a more abundant and fulfilling life for yourself . . . and then share that wealth with the world.

—**Jack Canfield**, Santa Barbara, California;
coauthor of the *Chicken Soup for the Soul®* series
and Featured Teacher in *The Secret*

PREFACE

....

*You have magic at your fingertips to manifest
anything you've ever wanted in a way that has never been
revealed to you . . . until now.*

—MONICA MAIN

....

Among the most sacred legends in the world is one that began in 1908 when an ambitious twenty-five-year old entrepreneur and wannabe writer named Oliver Napoleon Hill embarked on a lifelong mission to study hundreds of self-made millionaires. His efforts were prompted by Andrew Carnegie, a man whose name remains synonymous with great wealth and philanthropy. Not even halfway through the journey, in 1919, Carnegie passed away—it was too soon for him to witness the true genius of Napoleon Hill; what the business magnate and others *did* see at that time were mostly concealed and watered-down conclusions suitable for the times.

Nearly twenty years later, in 1937, the real findings of the secrets to success and riches were published in Hill's now-classic book *Think and Grow Rich*. It is said that upon its release, it was received as anything but a classic—in fact, the opposite was true. It was maligned, discredited, and soon removed from bookshelves through an initiative by some elites, such as Henry Ford, who wanted to ensure that the common man and woman would never know the truth behind untold wealth, health, and happiness. I think this hatchet job probably broke Hill's heart, who most likely believed that his life's work would always be altered and misrepresented by forces outside of his control—forces that wanted to keep the knowledge to themselves in order to keep their power, status, and fragile egos in place.

Since then, a number of charlatans promising the secrets of attracting great wealth—but delivering only fantasies—have cast shadows on *Think and Grow Rich*, proving, unfortunately, that the light of truth can be lost in the darkness of lies. There *is* a conspiracy working against you. It's not just your imagination, but it's also not in the way you may think.

For instance, not too long ago I discovered that a critical piece of information from Hill was being concealed from the masses. It is critical in the sense that it is the difference between your living an abundant and joyous life or struggling to find meaning in this seemingly chaotic wasteland. The very core of this gem has often been hidden from you by those who possess it—either by their ignorance or their maliciousness—though it could be argued that it is not an either/or, but rather that malicious individuals are also absurdly ignorant.

What emotion is driving them to do this? In a word: *fear.* They're afraid of people like you and me because we represent the masses, and we could rule the world if we came together in unity, easily conquering those who are in power now. They fear that if we were let inside their inner sanctums, they'd lose control over their billion-dollar companies and organizations, and their employees and customers; that is, people like you and me. They'd lose their control over parasitically profiting by first seducing us, then entangling us, and finally sticking it to us with chronic debt that keeps most of us slaves to their systems.

They spout big lies saying that there isn't enough money, love, and happiness for *everyone.* I'm here to tell you the opposite: *Yes, there is,* and it is available to anyone who wants to understand the science and inner workings of the laws of attraction. There's no need to withhold these tried-and-true principles. There's no meaningful benefit in stringing people along. Sure, there are superficial benefits for those who only reveal small bits of information at a time with the intent of profiting from selling more books, workshops, and movies. In the meantime, you, the student of these materials, become the one who suffers because you're given only a small part of the bigger picture. Without all the pieces, you cannot possibly manifest what you want in life. However, I'm here to help change that for you.

I believe that Napoleon Hill was sincere in his work and that his intentions were well placed. Basically, I believe he was truly a good man. So as I was writing this book, I began to wonder how his work was passed over by mainstream publishers, whom I also think were predominantly, and still are, basically noble professionals, and instead found its way to an obscure press named The Ralston Society (with some apparent affiliation with Ralston University Press in Meriden, Connecticut—both now long defunct).

What little we do know about Ralston is that the company gravitated toward books such as *Think and Grow Rich*, and published related works on the power of the human mind. Did it exist on the fringes for as long as it could before being run out of town, which is what happened to so many who were associated with Hill? Back then, in the 1930s, the power of the mind was magnificent, even if it remained mysterious. That was an era when radio was the primary form of entertainment—it harnessed Americans' attention with swing and Big Band music sandwiched between news, comedy, and dramatic shows. Automobile models were moving toward more luxury, and Cadillac was the "Standard of the World" for US technology. The power of the mind would also become apparent in a negative way as nations teetered on the brink of World War II.

What a completely different era we live in now! However, the desire to live a happy, joyous life remains a common thread throughout our nation's history. There's an important distinction to be made, though. Never before has the world been in more need of the critical lessons that Napoleon Hill offered, because never before has the world undergone such massive change in such a short period of time. The Information Age has brought about great advancements coupled with enormous chaos, displacement, disillusionment, and lack of control.

The Lost Secret can help give you some immediate relief from this confusion and also open doors to the big dreams you may have always had but haven't known how to manifest. Together, let's remove the mystery from these teachings, despite the risk of retribution and retaliation from those who want to keep this knowledge for themselves.

I believe Napoleon Hill's intentions were pure from the start. Then again, I don't know the full story, and perhaps I never will. But I know more of the story than I ever did, and you will, too, thanks to the discovery of Hill's lost teachings—two never-before-published chapters omitted, for whatever reason, from the original version of *Think and Grow Rich*.

May this book give you all the power, wisdom, and peace you deserve!

THE MYSTERY BEHIND HOW THIS SECRET CAME TO THE SURFACE

I once was lost but now I'm found,
was blind but now I see.

—JOHN NEWTON

One day I woke up and realized that my entire life was a lie. Or at least I felt that way. Call it a midlife crisis or whatever you want, but I knew deep inside that there had to be more than just "this." And if there wasn't more, I felt like I would want to jump off the nearest bridge to escape the dead end I was stuck in.

I was unhappy in every imaginable way. Strangely enough, from the outside looking in, it seemed that I had the perfect life. I was married, and I had a beautiful young daughter who was and still is the absolute light of my life. My company was outrageously successful, I lived in a beautiful home, and drove amazing luxury cars. Yet, from the inside looking out, life was far from perfect. To be completely honest, a lot was incredibly wrong with *everything.* The more *stuff* I acquired and the more success I experienced, the farther I drifted from feeling a sense of purpose and happiness. I felt more and more disconnected with each passing year.

I think a lot of people go through what I call the "moment," when you're moving along through life and then one day, *boom,* it occurs to you that maybe you've been heading in the wrong direction the whole time! Panic sets in, and you start to freak out because you've been going about your life in this way for so long that to change course at this point seems overwhelming, and nearly impossible to achieve.

If, like me, you've had this moment, you might have said to yourself, *What do I do now? Stay the current course and pretend I'm happy? After all, it seems to be working. Or do I go all in, put all my chips on the table, and risk everything for the chance to be blissfully happy?*

It was in the midst of my moment many years ago when I met a man named Roy. After a very long day of conferences and meetings, I had just taken a seat in the lounge at the hotel I was staying at. I was a pro at trekking through business trips, one after the other. Sure, it was always first-class this and that, but still, I was putting my body, mind, and spirit through such a beating. I remember sitting there and realizing that I had to start cutting back on these types of business trips. This was mostly because I missed not being home more to watch my young daughter grow up, but also because these trips had become too much of a burden, weighted down even more by what seemed like their increasing meaninglessness. I started to wonder if any of these trips were doing me good as far as furthering my business success. Deep down I doubted they were, so my thoughts shifted from cutting them back to cutting them out.

I sipped on my Grey Goose lemon-drop martini, one of my favorite drinks when I was on the road, set it down, and silently stared into the misty-yellow cocktail with a lemon slice so delicately and perfectly wedged on the rim of the glass. My thoughts grew deeper. I contemplated my next business move because I felt this couldn't go on; something had to give. I could literally see in my mind the words *DEAD END* spray-painted in red across dark, rickety boards nailed together. On the other side of that sign was a cliff, one that I felt I was only inches away from careening over, plummeting to the distant ground below, ending it all.

My third marriage was falling apart. My business—something I'd enjoyed with an absolute passion—was filling me with self-hate, and my excitement about waking up in the morning was replaced with a feeling of burnout beyond comprehension. I think I was only existing on the fumes from the adrenaline of my former powerhouse self. But I didn't even know where or how to begin sorting any of these things out because I was just too worn down, frazzled to the core, and despondent to think clearly.

Somewhere between my foggy thoughts of despair and toppling over a cliff, an older gentleman—maybe in his early eighties—sat two barstools to my right. I noticed his fluffy, cloud-like white hair as he laced his fingers together. The glimmer of an oversize gold ring with a bloodred garnet on the middle finger of his right hand also caught my eye. Was it a college ring? A football ring? I didn't know. On his left hand was a simple gold wedding band. He glanced over at me and smiled—the kind of smile meant to offer solace to someone who looked distraught. I politely smiled at him, then turned my attention back to nursing my martini.

"What do you think of the conference?" he asked, introducing himself as "Roy."

I shrugged. "Pretty much like the rest of 'em. Same stuff, different city."

"Oh, you go to a lot of these, do you?"

You have no idea, I thought. "A few here and there."

He nodded his understanding. After flagging down the bartender to order a burger with fries and a Coke, he picked up the conversation again. "So, what do you do?"

"I have my own publishing company. I self-publish my books, I have home-study courses, and I also do seminars and workshops."

"Hmm."

I thought maybe I hadn't revealed enough to have elicited only a "Hmm," so I added, "Mostly about investing."

He said, "My stepfather was in the publishing business. He worked for The Ralston Society. Ever heard of them?" He stirred the straw in his Coke, then moved it aside and took a drink straight from the glass.

I moved over one barstool so I didn't feel like I was shouting. The lounge was filling up with other weary and equally frazzled-looking conference attendees apparently eager to have drinks (lots of them) and dinner.

"Afraid not." I signaled to the bartender for my second round—I'd really come to love this form of nonverbal communication. "What's The Ralston Society?"

"They published *Think and Grow Rich* back in the 1930s. You've heard of *Think and Grow Rich* by Napoleon Hill, haven't you?"

I replied, "Of course, I have!" I was going to add, *Who hasn't?* but thought that might be disrespectful. "Every businessperson I know has read *Think and Grow Rich* at one time or another."

"My stepdad worked for The Ralston Society during that time." Roy started in on his burger and fries. He was a knife-and-fork man with that burger, but I wondered if maybe he used his hands when he wasn't at a five-star establishment.

The Grey Goose was starting to kick in about then, and I have to admit I don't remember all the specifics of the conversation after that point. But I do remember Roy talking about Napoleon Hill and an untold, unknown secret surrounding some of his writings, particularly tied to *Think and Grow Rich*. I remember Roy going on and on, in between his well-mannered consumption of burger and fries and my polite sips of my cocktail. I even remember my fascination with the artistically caked-on sugar on the rim of my glass as a side thought because I wasn't able to get a single word in edgewise.

At one point I must've decided that Roy was probably off his rocker, so I feigned an overwhelming sense of exhaustion coupled with a pounding headache, gave him my business card, and told him to email me with his address so I could send him some free books.

I never heard from him and forgot all about the incident—that is, until many years later in the weeks preceding the 2017 holiday season. This is when I received a mysterious email from someone who identified himself only as "R.C." He sent me a poorly written and extremely vague note about how he had some chapters from *Think and Grow Rich* that had never been published in the original 1937 edition. He went on to write that he'd send me a copy of the chapters in the mail. Not giving the whole thing much thought, I deleted the email without responding.

Shortly thereafter, I took a trip to the Big Island of Hawaii. The scenery at Anaeho'omalu Bay was, and always is, exquisite, but my mind was blocking the view, tugging at me: *What if there really were some Lost Chapters? What would they look like? How many chapters were there? What did they say? And why weren't they part of the original book published in the spring of 1937?*

Then I nodded off and had the most realistic, profound, and magical dream. I was in a very large room in a five-star hotel somewhere, getting dressed in a wedding gown on the verge of marrying one of my now ex-husbands. (Yes, there were three in total.) I was loathing the thought of marriage, not wanting to go through with it, but felt I had to for some reason.

I suddenly noticed a heavy burgundy velvet curtain. I drew it open, and there was the most beautiful ocean view as far as the eye could see. I saw a sidewalk right below the surface of the water, and gazed down farther to find a gentle tide ebbing and flowing, lapping at my toes, as if summoning me to follow. I began walking out on the sidewalk, which made it appear as though I were walking on water. It was a majestic feeling, one that spoke to me about having a whole new life ahead of me through which I could go anywhere I wanted to and become anyone I chose to be.

Then suddenly, this sense of fear hit me like a bolt of lightning, and in an instant turned into panic. *Where am I going? Does this sidewalk go on forever? Will I get lost in this ocean? Will I drown? I must go back!* At the moment I began to turn around to go back, I woke up from this dream.

I knew what it meant. It meant that trying to fit back into my former life in any way—whether it be a relationship or anything else—would hold me back forever. It meant that I needed to embrace the new life the Universe wanted to give me. I knew it was all there for the taking, yet my confidence was shaky. I didn't know if I'd be safe in the Universe on this journey into a new life.

When I had that dream, I was struggling with going back into an old relationship that wasn't working. They say that's the definition of insanity: doing the same thing over and over again yet expecting a different result. But that's exactly what I was doing—too afraid to let go of what was dragging me down and feeling miserable to the core.

Many of us do this very thing. We hang on to the old that clearly doesn't serve us because we're too scared of the unknown, even though, deep down, our hearts are telling us to take the leap.

I returned from Hawaii with a lot more questions, but also with a lot more answers. On December 30, the last Saturday of 2017, I'd gone to my office to make sure my fish were fed and to do a little work. On the floor, haphazardly stuffed through the office-door mail slot, I saw a crumpled-up manila envelope with my name and address scribbled on it with a barely legible black marker. The return address was from a post-office box in Chicago.

Could this be it? My heart was racing as I ripped open the envelope and found a note from a man named Roy Chamberlain. I instantly knew he was the "R.C." from the email. Roy began by reiterating what he'd told me in the hotel lounge: that his step-father had worked for The Ralston Society, the publisher of *Think and Grow Rich*––and that at some point before going to press, it was decided by the editor or publisher to delete chapters 16 and 17 from the book. No explanation was offered as to why, and *Think and Grow Rich* went on to be published with only fifteen chapters.

We can only speculate as to why the two chapters were left out. Was it because of page-count constraints? Did the chapters contain information that The Ralston Society felt the general public wasn't ready for? Did those chapters make too little sense in the context of the rest of the book? Were these the only chapters left out, or could there be more? Were these Lost Chapters even real, or were they fakes?

In his note, Roy further explained that he'd intended on doing something with these chapters, but time had gotten away from him . . . and so had his memory. He wrote that he'd forgotten that he had the Lost Chapters, and when he'd come upon them recently, he realized that at this stage in his life, he wasn't up to disseminating them to the public, at least not on his own. That's where *I* came into the picture. At the end of his note, he wrote: "I trust that you'll know what to do with these."

Upon analyzing these Lost Chapters, I knew that I hadn't been given the original documents. The ones I had were barely legible copies of what I can only assume were the originals. I can also only assume that Roy had kept the originals because they were much too valuable to mail off to a complete stranger.

I was unsuccessful in recovering his deleted email. My other attempts to contact Roy have also been futile. All I have is a post-mark from Chicago with an invalid return address. I even hired a private detective to track Roy down, but he, too, found nothing.

After reading those two chapters repeatedly, I felt that the way they were written was remarkably similar to how Napoleon Hill had expressed himself through the many books he wrote, including, and especially, *Think and Grow Rich*.

I understand that it might be tempting for you, the reader, to want to skip ahead now to the end of this book and just read those two final chapters, but I urge you not to do so—mainly because you'll miss out on the context in which they're presented, which is necessary to determine their authenticity. However, I understand that you might sometimes want to eat dessert before having the main course. If that's the case, you can jump ahead to chapters 16 and 17 and read the Lost Chapters, but you should only do so if you've already read *Think and Grow Rich* and understand Hill's basic principles. Be sure, though, to return to the beginning and read this entire book to gain a much deeper appreciation for those Lost Chapters.

I'm certain that these are the missing chapters from the original manuscript, but ultimately, you'll have to decide for yourself. Most important, you'll have to determine if the information in chapters 16 and 17 can change the trajectory of your life, because I already know the answer to that: they *can* and they *will* if you'll just *apply* them over and over again. I'm hoping that you can get everything you've ever wanted and more in this life, and that's why I've taken such a huge risk on so many levels—namely, legally and financially—to bring you these Lost Chapters.

Chapter One

CAN ANYONE REALLY "THINK AND GROW RICH"?

....

Concentrate on the things you want, not on the things you do not want.

—CHARLES F. HAANEL

....

The first time I touched a copy of *Think and Grow Rich* was in the spring of 1984. I was a few weeks shy of my tenth birthday, and my family had just moved into my grandma's house after yet another one of my father's businesses failed. We'd run out of money to pay rent for our home in Panama City, Florida, and with nowhere else to go, back to the Chicago suburbs and into Grandma's house we went.

My brother, Jason, and I shared a room for the year and a half or so we were there. It wasn't a typical room—two doors on each side acted more like a pass-through than an actual bedroom. As I understood it, back in the 1950s, it was popular for developers to sell people a "shell." (They call them "vanilla shells" nowadays.) It's essentially just a house with four walls on a slab of concrete. It was up to the new owners to build the interior, and that's what my grandfather did . . . though not very well, which I thought was strange for someone who was a draftsman and a government engineer. But in all fairness, he made no claims to being an architect.

In this room there was a closet that stuck out awkwardly. It didn't take long for my brother and me to become curious about it because it had all kinds of cool things that were supposed to be off-limits to us. Naturally, when you're a kid, being told *no* makes the intrigue all that much greater. Even when Grandma would yell when she caught us rummaging through that closet, that only served to turn our curiosity into an obsession. With each passing day, we got better at playing the game of scouting around in there without getting caught.

The closet had such a distinct aroma to it that to this day, I recall it whenever I even think about opening that door. The muskiness was mostly from my grandfather's oil paintings and other art supplies, and records of his long-lost dreams that he'd never followed through on. There were also books, magazines, run-of-the-mill junk, folded paper grocery bags, and little "treasures" tucked in there for safekeeping.

On the left middle shelf was a neatly stacked pile of books. The book on the very top was *Think and Grow Rich*. It had lost its dust jacket somewhere along the way, so it boldly revealed the title printed across the front binding and a cute trio of a top hat, cane, and pair of gloves at the bottom. That little image still remains burned into my brain because it *really* attracted my attention.

The original *Think and Grow Rich* cover from 1937.

When I opened the book, I asked myself some daunting questions: *Can somebody just "think and grow rich"? Is this remotely possible? If so, how can I "think and grow rich" too?*

Up to that point in my young life, I'd only experienced poverty. I realize now that this was when resentment about my circumstances began to grow; this resentment would later become the rocket fuel for my *burning desire* to become rich, no matter what.

Over the next few years, as I entered my teens and twenties, I would pick up *Think and Grow Rich* time and time again but struggled to make much progress with each sincere attempt to read it. I found the words of Napoleon Hill to be as dry as dust and boring beyond description. I would constantly ask myself, *What the hell do people see in this book?*

It wasn't until I got into my forties that I began to really appreciate *Think and Grow Rich*. I had attended a seminar where there was an auction for an original first edition of the book. The second I saw it, I instantly thought back to when I was nine years old and first laid eyes on that top hat, cane, and gloves; I could even smell the old oil paint and turpentine in my grandparents' closet once again. I knew right then that I had to bid on the book. And not only did I plan to bid on it, but I was determined to acquire it, no matter the cost.

The auction was held to raise money for two charities that took care of abandoned farm animals. Although there were quite a few highly valuable items up for auction, I was surprised that no one else had put in a bid for this "treasure." I kept checking to see if anybody else had upped the bid over the entire three-day event. But no, not a peep, and I acquired the book for only $750. For me, this is when the magic began.

My precious book remained in its plastic case for safekeeping. I looked at it for several days, wondering if it would be okay to read from a more than eighty-year-old work that had existed on this planet nearly twice as long as I had. A week later I finally made up my mind to go ahead and carefully crack open the cover a few times here and there, to test whether I should dare handle it. Each time I did, some of the pages looked like they could fall out at any moment. But its age intrigued me further, and I felt that the secrets it contained called to me. So slowly and very carefully, I began to read this old book.

It wasn't long before I was put off by Napoleon Hill's dated and heavily male-laden language. It was of the times, meaning that it was all about "men"—a word sometimes interchanged with the singular "man," though once in a blue moon Hill would throw in a "women" or "woman." It was obvious that he had discounted women, who were largely viewed in those days as baby makers and housewives.

Regardless, the further I dove in to the material, the more I extracted from it. At the end of the book, I came away with the same deduction that I'd intuitively known as that nine-year-old little girl so many years before. You can't just "think" and grow rich. You also have to "do" something along with your thinking. However, the process does start with the spark of a thought—even a small one—that can begin to churn the powers that shape both the seen and the unseen. As Napoleon Hill wrote in *Think and Grow Rich*:

> Truly, "thoughts are things," and powerful things at that, when they are mixed with definiteness of purpose, persistence, and a BURNING DESIRE for their translation into riches or other material objects.

⟨═══⟩

Author Earl Nightingale, who was deeply inspired by Napoleon Hill, said, "We become what we think about most of the time, and that is the strangest secret." Let me explain: While you're moving along in life, you'll tend to think about how you're doing based on the environment you're in. If it's not the life you ultimately want, one secret is to think differently so that you create a new environment that will foster the life you desire. Of course, this can be difficult to do because the more you're immersed in life the way it is, it "wires" your brain to accept this as a permanent reality. The "trick," of course, it to find ways to override your reality, which I'll cover later on.

What most people don't know is that Hill's publisher had insisted that his book be called *Use Your Noodle and Get the Boodle* (true!). Fortunately for all of us, the author used *the power of the ether* to create a new title at the last minute: *Think and Grow Rich*. I say *fortunately* because any book with "noodle" and "boodle" in the title isn't one I would pick up, unless of course it was a children's book. I'm also doubtful that *noodles and boodles* would have drawn in the more than seventy million people in total who've bought this treasure. Besides, the whole idea surrounding *Think and Grow Rich* is to use the power of your mind to create whatever you want. Yes, you really do have this power! The key is to find a way to focus on the new life you want while existing in the old environment you're currently in. This is where things get tricky, which is likely why Hill went to great lengths to describe the phenomenal story of a man named Edwin C. Barnes:

> A little more than thirty years ago, Edwin C. Barnes discovered how true it is that men really do THINK AND GROW RICH. His discovery did not come about at one sitting. It came little by little, beginning with a BURNING DESIRE to become a business associate of the great Edison.
>
> One of the chief characteristics of Barnes' Desire was that it was *definite*. He wanted to work with Edison, not *for* him. Observe, carefully, the description of how he went about translating his DESIRE into reality, and you will have a better understanding of the thirteen principles which lead to riches.
>
> When this DESIRE, or impulse of thought, first flashed into his mind he was in no position to act upon it. Two difficulties stood in his way. He did not know Mr. Edison, and he did not have enough money to pay his railroad fare to Orange, New Jersey.
>
> These difficulties were sufficient to have discouraged the majority of men from making any attempt to carry out the desire. But his was no ordinary desire! He was so determined to find a way to carry out his desire that he finally decided to travel by "blind baggage," rather than be defeated. (To the

uninitiated, this means that he went to East Orange on a freight train.)

He presented himself at Mr. Edison's laboratory, and announced he had come to go into business with the inventor. In speaking of the first meeting between Barnes and Edison, years later, Mr. Edison said, *"He stood there before me, looking like an ordinary tramp, but there was something in the expression of his face which conveyed the impression that he was determined to get what he had come after.* I had learned, from years of experience with men, that when a man really DESIRES a thing so deeply that he is willing to stake his entire future on a single turn of the wheel in order to get it, he is sure to win. I gave him the opportunity he asked for, *because I saw he had made up his mind to stand by until he succeeded.* Subsequent events proved no mistake was made."

Just what young Barnes said to Mr. Edison on that occasion was far less important than *that which he thought.* It was what he THOUGHT that counted.

One sound idea is all that one needs to achieve success. The principles described in this book, contain the best, and the most practical of all that is known, concerning ways and means of creating useful ideas.

Before we go any further in our approach to the description of these principles, we believe you are entitled to receive this important suggestion . . . WHEN RICHES BEGIN TO COME THEY COME SO QUICKLY, IN SUCH GREAT ABUNDANCE, THAT ONE WONDERS WHERE THEY HAVE BEEN HIDING DURING ALL THOSE LEAN YEARS. This is an astounding statement, and all the more so, when we take into consideration the popular belief, that riches come only to those who work hard and long.

Success comes to those who become SUCCESS CONSCIOUS.

Failure comes to those who indifferently allow themselves to become FAILURE CONSCIOUS.

The object of this book is to help all who seek it, to learn the art of changing their minds from FAILURE CONSCIOUSNESS to SUCCESS CONSCIOUSNESS.

Ideas and Inspirations—Where Do They Come From?

Exactly where do these thoughts and ideas of inspiration come from in the first place? How did Barnes find the gumption to present his rather grandiose and outrageous ideas to Edison?

The answer is what makes this entire secret to be like that of a complete circle—you cannot describe how it begins without first attempting to describe how it ends. That's how I found *Think and Grow Rich* to be—start off with your thoughts, but don't expound on precisely where that big idea will initially come from.

The truth is, many of us are geniuses in our own right, but that's not how the "big ideas" come to fruition. They don't come from remembered and processed information that you've collected over the years. In reality, your boldest, broadest, biggest, and best ideas don't come from your brain at all. As we move ahead, I'll reveal exactly where they *do* come from . . . and it may surprise you!

Chapter Two

THE FIRST STEP TOWARD RICHES: WHAT IS YOUR BURNING DESIRE?

....

Once you make a decision, the Universe conspires to make it happen.

—RALPH WALDO EMERSON

....

When I was twelve years old, I wanted to move from Panama City, Florida, to Hollywood to become an actress. This became my *burning desire* or *chief aim*, which no other desire could compete with. Day and night I thought of moving to Southern California. I visualized it in the morning when I woke up, and even bought a map of the area that I tacked to the wall in my bedroom. It was one of those Los Angeles souvenirs that showed the most famous tourist attractions and landmarks from the Hollywood sign to the Capitol Records building. During the day, I studied it, meticulously memorizing every street, landmark, and building until I knew them all by heart. Each night I fell asleep with this vision implanted in my mind and in the pit of my stomach.

My focus didn't include much about what I'd do once I landed. All I really cared about was just getting to Southern California. Unbeknownst to me as a precocious twelve-year-old were the many real-world obstacles, including my parents' financial inability to relocate our family; and even if by some miracle they did have the money, they didn't have any connection to the area or any interest in it other than what they saw on TV or in the movies. However, I desired this specific geographical change to the West Coast so much that I could taste it. I just *knew* it would happen, some way, somehow. And guess what? *Less than six months later, we moved to Southern California.*

The move came about through a series of "mysterious" and abrupt events that could not have possibly been planned. One moment we were going to move back to Chicago where we were from; the next moment we were moving to California because my uncle decided to relocate there, which prompted my dad to follow. That was back in 1987, and I've been here ever since.

That was my first experience of what it was like to *deliberately create and manifest* what I wanted from nothing more than a *burning desire*. While I never became an actress—mostly because I realized later on through drama classes that I didn't like acting—the power of creation wasn't lost on me. Unfortunately, though, I chose for decades thereafter to sweep this immense power of creation under the rug. Fortunately, I chose to come back to it. Or, rather, this incredible Source Energy made the *decision* for me.

I realize now that being immature, having a lack of life experience, and being a "delusional" little kid worked completely in my favor. If I'd known all the "realities" that were stacked against me, I would have talked myself out of this desire, in the same way my grandfather gave up on his art. My dream would have never manifested itself, likely ending up in a metaphorical musty closet along with Grandpa's acrylics, canvases, and paintbrushes.

I believe it's about time that all of us find ways to be "delusional" little kids with big dreams who recognize limitations or obstacles but do not accept them!

Desire: The Key Starting Point to All Manifestation

The word *desire* comes from the Latin words *de sire*, which mean "of the father." Your desires—whether viewed as easy or seemingly difficult to acquire, as possible or impossible—have already been given to you from a higher place. No desire would even be bestowed upon you if there wasn't a possibility for its attainment. So along with your desires, you're also given action plans, ideas, and inspirations to follow in order to get what you want out of life.

In the story about the Edison/Barnes partnership, it began with Barnes first *desiring* a significant improvement in his finances. Then the *thought* about working with Edison was sent to him as a burst of inspiration *requiring* his follow-through. It was Barnes's persistent action and willingness to be flexible in dealing with whatever came about that was key to his success. If he'd sat and let the ideas, thoughts, and plans given to him just rattle around in his brain without taking any action, he might have lived a very unhappy existence.

"Action is the foundational key to all success." This quote from Pablo Picasso leads me to believe that "think and grow rich" is actually a misnomer. Napoleon Hill outlined how it was beyond just "rich thinking" that was responsible for Barnes's success. He was determined to visit Edison because he was determined to get to the place he'd envisioned for himself. He didn't give up at any point. It's likely that giving up wasn't even an option in his mind. He acted based on the energy from his burning desire. This is the key point here, so I will repeat it: He acted based on the energy from his burning desire.

Without a Burning Desire, You Cannot Manifest Anything

All manifestation must start with a burning desire. You'd be shocked, though, to find out how many people don't have a wisp of an idea of what they really want out of life and wonder why they don't have the life they want. As the Cheshire Cat in *Alice in Wonderland* says, "If you don't know where you are going, any road will take you there."

On the flip side, just about everybody understands that when they go to a restaurant for breakfast, they need to be crystal clear about placing their order: eggs over easy, medium, or hard; with sourdough, wheat, or rye toast; and a side of bacon, sausage, or ham. So if you're not precise when placing your order for what you want in life, don't be surprised if you're served something you want to send back to the kitchen!

Let's break this down. The reason you don't know exactly what you want is probably because you're allowing others to influence you, or even dictate what you do and do not want. Your head is foggy with everybody else's ideas and plans about how you should live your life and what you should be doing. Some of this programming took place in your childhood—maybe your dad said you'd be better off getting an accounting degree instead of being a musician, like you really wanted to do. Other programming is taking place every day as you scan your phone for the latest disaster or look on Instagram to see what your friends just posted. Or sometimes you take social cues from people and unconsciously conform. The takeaway here is if you aren't stingy about how you devote your attention, including whom you spend your time with, then the media, your friends and family, advertisers, and so on will take your attention and spend it the way they see fit.

To manifest something with absolute certainty, you'll need your own burning desire. So, what's the difference between a run-of-the-mill desire and a burning desire? Napoleon Hill made the answer clear:

> *A BURNING DESIRE is not a hope! It is not a wish! It is a keen, pulsating DESIRE, which transcends everything else because of your willingness to do whatever it takes to make it happen. THAT is the difference between a lukewarm desire and a BURNING DESIRE.*

What is *your* passion? What do you want more than anything? Your burning desire forces manifestation to go to the next level, even before you need to act upon it. Hill highlighted this crucial understanding at a particular point in his story about Barnes:

As [Barnes] made his way from the railroad tracks to Thomas A. Edison's office, his mind was at work. He saw himself *standing in Edison's presence*. He heard himself asking Mr. Edison for an opportunity to carry out the one CONSUMING OBSESSION OF THIS LIFE, a BURNING DESIRE to become the business associate of the great inventor.

Barnes' desire was not a <u>hope</u>! It was not a <u>wish</u>! It was a keen, pulsating DESIRE, which transcended everything else. It was DEFINITE.

The desire was not new when he approached Edison. It had been Barnes' *dominating desire* for a long time. In the beginning, when the desire first appeared in his mind, it may have been, probably was, only a wish, but it was no mere wish when he appeared before Edison with it.

Barnes succeeded because he chose a definite goal, placed all his energy, all his will power, all his effort, everything back of that goal. He did not become the partner of Edison the day he arrived. He was content to start in the most menial work, as long as it provided an opportunity to take even one step toward his cherished goal.

It is a remarkable illustration of the power of a DEFINITE DESIRE. Barnes won his goal, because he wanted to be a business associate of Mr. Edison, more than he wanted anything else. He created a plan by which to attain that purpose. But he BURNED ALL BRIDGE BEHIND HIM. He stood by his DESIRE until it became the dominating obsession of his life—and—finally, a fact.

He left himself no possible way of retreat. He had to win or perish!

Every person who wins any undertaking must be willing to burn his ships and cut all sources of retreat. Only by doing so can one be sure of maintaining the state of mind known as a BURNING DESIRE TO WIN, essential to success.

Where Does a Burning Desire Come From?

Napoleon Hill did not say exactly *where* a burning desire comes from; however, he suggested that it's already within you. For instance, in referring to Barnes, he said: "It came little by little, beginning with a BURNING DESIRE to become a business associate of the great Edison."

Does this mean Barnes rolled out of bed one day and just randomly began thinking about business partnerships with someone famous? From out of the blue, with no precursors?

Or was the *origin* of his idea—his *inspiration*—from somewhere else, based on wanting, energetically lining up, and being ready for some kind of major change in his life? Perhaps the idea was through the "ether," as Hill describes it, although I prefer the term *Source Energy* or the *Universe*—based on the ambitious entrepreneur already having some-yet-to-be-clarified deep-rooted desire for change within himself. Perhaps that's the instant when thoughts of inspiration arrived from Source Energy, and those sparks powered Barnes to follow through with action to make the change he craved. My belief is that the "what" comes first—financial freedom, a loving relationship, a sense of purpose—and the "how" comes second.

Earlier, I mentioned all the people who don't know what they want, and because of that, they remain unhappy. And then there are the people who *do* know what they want but don't know how to achieve it; they *also* remain unhappy throughout their lives.

Chances are you can personally relate to these individuals. The way out of the fog is to open your mind and heart, starting with raising your energy and vibrational levels to match the vibrations to which your burning-desire "particles" of thought and inspiration can be attracted.

You can add another simple element: *ask.* "Ask and it will be given to you; seek and you will find; knock and the door will be opened to you" (Matthew 7:7). Once you open yourself up by *aligning* to this Source Energy, then pay attention to the nuggets of inspiration and ideas that could lead to opportunities for attaining your desire.

When we consistently raise our vibrational energies to a high-enough level, we become the transmitting beam to thousands, if not millions, of inspirational thoughts that we can convert into currency here and now. By currency, I mean monetarily capitalizing on those thoughts of inspiration that fuel your burning desire. This could be in the form of an invention or reorganization, or perhaps in the form of a piece of music or other type of artwork. The opportunities are endless.

Not only do you have to increase your vibrational energy to start to see these opportunities; you must also "rewire" your brain to see what you may be automatically overlooking all the time. You will also have to dismiss all the negativity and doubt that can overcome you when it comes to attaining your greatest desires. Yes, you have to "train" yourself to see the glass as half-full instead of half-empty, train yourself to see solutions instead of obstacles, and train yourself to see setbacks as teachers instead of failures. If you train yourself to rise above negativity from every avenue it flies at you—from the mass media to your own disparaging self-talk—and only focus on positivity, you can command and manifest everything you want.

Please let me explain some of the basic mechanics, which can be described in even more detail through quantum physics. When you come into alignment with a higher vibrational energy, you begin to line up with all things that exist on that level. This includes love, abundance, happiness, optimal health, bliss, and much more. It's just not possible to be sad or impoverished in thinking and feeling when you're vibrating at this higher level, because low vibes and high vibes *never* mesh together at one time. Therefore, the ideal scenario is to constantly feel yourself vibrating at the highest energy level possible. This will keep the "bad" thoughts away, including debilitating doubts and irrational fears. It's only when you vibrate at lower levels that you'll find yourself worrying, panicking, obsessing, giving up, and, well, you can fill in the rest of this very long list.

If Others Can Do It, So Can You!

One thing about our current Information Age is that we can instantly see how wealthy people live. We can Google pictures of their mansions and luxury cars. We can read about rags-to-riches millionaires and billionaires. We can vicariously experience their success. This gives us a great advantage in aligning our own thinking to match those of prosperous individuals.

A hundred years ago in the Agrarian Age, and then through much of the Industrial Age, if people were brought up in poverty and despair, their thoughts and ideas would most probably *match* poverty and despair for the rest of their lives. Their lower vibrational energies aligned with their environments, reflecting lack and limited means. While they may have had dreams of riches and success, the path to attain it was almost nonexistent. This is why the wealthy would marry other people of wealth throughout the ages. It wasn't so much about networking among others of great wealth (although that certainly was part of it), but it was mostly to ensure that the vibrational frequency of what they believed was in their DNA would be passed down to their offspring to guarantee wealth for generations to come.

How is it, then, that some people pull themselves up from being brought up in impoverished circumstances to reach the heights of great success? The answer is the same one we've been discussing all along. Despite their environments, at some point they came to *believe* that a better life was attainable for them. On some level—conscious or subconscious—they knew that breaking out of a life of destitution was possible, not just for themselves but for everyone in their families.

Here's a related example. Many times throughout modern history when there was an effort to break a record or reach a new milestone, it would take years to accomplish. But once it was done, in a short amount of time, others would meet or exceed that performance. Why is this? Well, it seems that we often need role models to first "prove" that something can be done before "people like us" can *believe* it can be done?

For women, there had to be the first female to run a successful multimillion-dollar business. Then a multibillion-dollar one. There had to be the first female to direct a major motion picture. Then one who ran a major movie studio. There had to be a first female who ran for mayor. Then one who ran for president. For those from a difficult upbringing, especially those who grew up in impoverished circumstances, there had to be a first who achieved success.

In these instances and so many more, these individuals' accomplishments ultimately gave thousands of others the *seedling of an idea* that the same kind of success was possible for them as well. It's through these "firsts" that many others could truly believe that bigger and better things were possible. But make no mistake: to be a "first" is a difficult endeavor and requires a lot of creative thinking to move beyond traditions, culture, and environment.

Are You a "Chosen One"?

What kind of person becomes a "chosen one," with the first *big idea*?

The answer is that we are *all* chosen. What you probably don't realize is that you beat tremendous odds just by being born and enjoying the body you're living in today. The process of being a fertilized egg and growing inside a mother's womb, in and of itself, is miraculous, regardless of what kind of life follows. Billions of acts on many physical and ethereal levels had to occur for you to be born; billions more had to occur for you to have made it where you are, in this moment, reading this book right now.

Go ahead and actively engage in those billions of acts to create what you *want* rather than leaving it to chance. You *already have* all the power and energy you need *right now* as a teeming biological and spiritual organism.

When you *know* you're destined for bigger, better things, you no longer have to scrounge around for ideas. Instead, you'll have a deep sense of what you'd like your next big move to be. You *already know* what you're aiming for, and are confident that the Universe is waiting for your bull's-eye. *That* is the big idea. *You* are the big idea. It's all about creating your destiny. So go ahead and embark on the journey you've been contemplating for far too long!

Just by taking the action of walking a different path—even if it turns out to be the wrong one—you'll be given new ideas and thoughts of inspiration to correct your course by further aligning yourself with Source Energy. The key is to take action based on those initial idea sparks and exciting nuggets when they're gifted to you. Once you get rolling, as long as you're connected to Source Energy through a higher vibrational energy, you'll always know that you're being guided toward your north star. You will *never* be sent in the wrong direction.

Artists refer to this as finding their muse. Others call it being in the *flow*. It's where time ceases to exist, and all the ideas you want or need come out. We all need these aligning thoughts, ideas, and inspirations that stem from a higher place. The good news is that we all can get to this place relatively quickly. To do so, we need to begin by focusing on something we really want. The idea may start out as something vague, such as a change in career. Or it could be something very specific, like wanting to attract a lifelong romantic partner. Either way, it must begin with a burning desire from within.

Let's say you have a clear vision of what you want but don't know the specifics of how to attain it. That's okay. Your seedling of desire is enough to get you started, and the *how* will be given to you as you move forward.

Many know what their life purpose is when they're around six or seven years old. Yet, for a good number of these people, as they grow up, they step out of alignment with their destiny. If you don't remember what *your* life purpose is, or remember it but don't know how to get beyond your doubts, I will help you by asking you to really try to remember this: What was your big dream at about six years old? Go deeper. Do you remember it now?

Once your burning desire has been established, and once your belief in its attainment comes to full bloom, ideas of inspiration will begin to flow into your mind. Maybe this will happen in the wee hours of the morning, or maybe while feeding ducks at a pond. Suddenly you'll exclaim, "Eureka! That's my big idea!" You'll *just know* it's the next move you need to make.

Or, let's say you don't know exactly what you want but you have a vague idea. Maybe you know you want to be wealthy but have no clue how to get there. That's also okay—not only okay, but quite common. An overall vision of what you want is enough to get you prepped for the ideas that will flow into your mind at just the right time. For instance, if one of your burning desires is to experience wealth—even if you're struggling financially right now—your *seedling of desire* is enough to spark a fire. You'll start to believe that you deserve to have your burning desire, and that you do, in fact, already have the ability to manifest it. Fine-tuning your way into alignment with Source Energy will then bring you the thoughts of inspiration and ideas you need to take action.

How to Attract Fast Money into Your Life

Worrying about how your burning desire is going to materialize often occurs when you believe your idea seems far-fetched. For example, say you want to manifest $100,000 in thirty days. But if you've never made more than $30,000 a year, deep down you might not really *believe* that attracting quick money like this is possible for you; and so, doubt, resistance, and cynicism will undermine your natural ability to create this manifestation.

On the flip side, if you've been a rap star for the past dozen years, have fallen on hard times, but you've had experiences where you were given $100,000 checks—regardless of what's going on in your life right now—you *believe* that attracting that level of income in a short time is a possibility for you based on your past experience. It's all in what you *believe* is possible for you that makes or breaks your success.

If having a specific dollar amount in mind is the trigger that keeps setting up your internal resistance, try *not* naming a specific dollar amount, and never think about how it will manifest. Just let the Universe sort through the details and trust that it'll all work out for you.

Also, when doing your visualizations about money, *feel the income* as if you're in flow with it. Money is nothing but a form of energy. You may say, "But, Monica, it's *not* energy. When I grab my wallet and take out a twenty, it's feels like grubby paper to me." Yes, I get it. But when you give money to someone, it's in exchange for a product or service. So, the money you give is a form of energy to get something in return that is of value to you. What you get in return is also a form of energy, whether it is a product, service, form of gratitude, or something else.

This is why robbers never really "get away" with stealing. If you aren't offering something of an *equal or greater energy level* as the person who's giving you the money, an energy imbalance forms. The Universe always corrects imbalances. In the case of criminals, they will usually lose the money, lose a portion of their life sitting behind bars, lose loved ones, or lose in some other way as *reimbursement* to the Universe for the imbalance in energy they're accountable for.

However, when you visualize money in a way that raises your vibrational level, you're simultaneously creating the necessary balance of energy output to receive the money you're summoning. If you happen to win the lottery after some energy-raising work, so be it—just keep your energy up there so that you can hold on to the winnings and not blow them, as so many lottery winners do.

To further avoid any resistance you may have to receiving money—particularly a dollar amount that you're not used to—it's critical that you (1) *view* money as a form of energy that requires you to be in a high vibratory state; (2) *imagine* yourself in the *flow* with money as if it's a river; (3) *know* that money is coming into your life; and (4) *love* money for the choices it gives you. Once you do all the above, you must then let go without fretting or doubting that the money will manifest . . . otherwise, it won't. You'll block its arrival with those kinds of attitudes and feelings—your high-vibe valve will close, and the money will have no clear path into your bank account.

Most important, know that, like all human beings, *you deserve unlimited abundance*, now and forever. This abundance is there for the taking. You can choose to take a thimble full of wealth from this roaring river of prosperity. Or you can choose to take a thousand large warehouses full of wealth from this same river. Either way, it will not affect the level of available abundance to you and others since it constantly regenerates itself. This abundance is available to you at all times. The Universe loves you and wants only the best for you. Embrace this unconditional love and abundance. Once you get out of your own way, these gifts are yours for the taking!

Take Immediate Action on Your Thoughts of Inspiration

"Thinking" to grow rich is only the very beginning of the process to manifest your burning desire. Like Barnes did when he scraped together the funds to hop on a train to meet Edison, you will also be required to take inspired action. There isn't any reason why you can't succeed, provided that you follow through with the *guided action* given through Source Energy.

The Six Steps for Getting What You Want

According to Napoleon Hill in *Think and Grow Rich*, there are six steps to start the process of getting what you want:

> **First.** Fix in your mind the exact amount of money you desire. It is not sufficient merely to say "I want plenty of money." Be definite as to the amount.
>
> **Second.** Determine exactly what you intend to give in return for the money you desire. (There is no such reality as "something for nothing.")
>
> **Third.** Establish a definite date when you intend to possess the money you desire.

Fourth. Create a definite plan for carrying out your desire, and begin *at once*, whether you are ready or not, to put this plan into *action*.

Fifth. Write out a clear, concise statement of the amount of money you intend to acquire, name the time limit for this acquisition, state what you intend to give in return for the money, and describe clearly the plan through which you intend to accumulate it.

Sixth. Read your written statement aloud, twice daily, once just before retiring at night, and once after arising in the morning. AS YOU READ—SEE AND FEEL AND BELIEVE YOURSELF ALREADY IN POSSESSION OF THE MONEY.

There is a difference between WISHING for a thing and being READY to receive it. No one is *ready* for a thing, until he believes he can acquire it. The state of mind must be BELIEF, not mere hope or wish. Open-mindedness is essential for belief. Closed minds do not inspire faith, courage, and belief.

⟺══⟹

The Zone

It takes no more effort to have what you *do* want than it does to have what you *don't* want, and the easiest way to attain your goal is to be in a high vibratory state. I call this being in the *Zone*. The more you keep yourself there, the more awesomeness will flow into your life.

"But, Monica," you may say, "it might be easy for you, but I'm dying over here. I can't catch a break."

And I would answer, "There's a good reason why. It's because most of us have our heads in the gutter a lot of the time, especially when we waste time. Imagine if we instantly got whatever we thought about; now recall all the terrible news you've read, watched, or heard in the past twenty-four hours. If we instantly got whatever we thought about, then we'd instantly attract war, corruption, crime, and all kinds of tragedies. Be grateful that it takes longer for the things you think about to come to fruition."

What this means is that you're required to completely disconnect from all things that bring your mind down. *Stop* watching the news. *Stop* visiting social media websites—in fact, you might want to consider deleting all your social medial accounts! *Stop* playing violent video games and participating in anything else that is negatively holding your thoughts hostage at lower vibratory levels. In order to have control over your thoughts, you must first gain control over your mind. That requires you to reprogram your mind, in large part by paying careful attention to what you focus on each and every day. If you're not willing to do so, your journey will end here.

Chapter Three

THE SECOND STEP TOWARD RICHES: UNWAVERING FAITH THROUGH JUST "KNOWING"

Faith is taking the first step even when you don't see the whole staircase.

—DR. MARTIN LUTHER KING JR.

From the time I was a tween, I always *knew* I'd be rich. I didn't know exactly how I'd get there, but I was certain I'd be a business-woman, and a shrewd one at that.

I remember arguing with my dad, asking him why he wouldn't start a successful business and make more money for us. He had an endless amount of excuses, but the one I remember most is when he'd say, "You need money to make money."

I'd push back, saying, "But, Dad, you only need a few hundred dollars to start a business. Just get started and build up from there." The more I brought up these arguments, the more he resisted; first by insisting it wasn't a possibility, and soon after by shutting me out.

I always knew it was possible to start a business with only a few hundred dollars, and I always knew I could be successful at doing it. Somehow I'd captured this strong belief as a young adult despite my impoverished surroundings.

Fast-forward about a decade, when I started my first business with only a few hundred dollars and turned it into a multimillion-dollar enterprise within months. Admittedly, in the beginning I set it up incorrectly, which resulted in a bunch of headaches. The fact of the matter is, I achieved what I believed: I could start with only a few hundred dollars and create a multimillion-dollar business. And I've done it several times more since then!

Even today, with my current successful businesses, I still exist on pure belief and faith. To be honest, I see my success over the years as a remarkable phenomenon, especially since I can get in my own way, just as many of us do at times. For example, when I'm pushing hard with new marketing campaigns, a lot of speaking engagements, and running around frazzled, doing the things I think I'm *supposed* to be doing for my business to stay successful, my money influx suffers. This, in turn, makes me feel stressed out, overwhelmed, worried for the future, and exhausted. This is also when I attract more "bad apples" who become thorns in my side. All this negativity churning inside gets mirrored on the outside, and my business does even worse.

On the other hand, when I do less, stay calm, and accept whatever happens, then everything seems to work out phenomenally well. In fact, during those times, I have more business than ever, work with kind and grateful people, and have more money flowing in—*while doing much less.*

Central to this remarkable phenomenon is a deep knowing that without any shadow of a doubt, things will all work out, no matter what. This deep knowing is one of a number of *secrets* behind why my businesses do incredibly well, and this same deep knowing can be applied to every aspect of life.

Hakuna matata! No worries! That's a great credo to live by.

What Is Faith?

Truth be told, I dislike the common perception of the word *faith* because it suggests a feeling of blindly hoping that something will come to fruition. It suggests that you've been reduced to throwing your heart out there with the hope that some white-bearded man in the clouds will respond to your yearnings. It suggests that what you want *might* happen but probably *won't*.

Many of us attempt to control every facet of our lives. We assume that we can control most things except for those we deem to be "accidents." The reality is, the only things we can personally control are our thoughts, and the *feeling vibrations* that are behind those thoughts. But if we think about it, controlling our thoughts and feelings is *absolutely everything* when it comes to creating what we want in life.

The reason you don't have the things you've always wanted in your life is because you *doubted* those dreams away. Yes, doubt overcame the faith that your dreams were coming. Doubt "sold" you on the belief that there was no way you could attain your desire, and that belief turned into the fact that your desire never manifested. In a sense, you succeeded—though not in the way you intended. You succeeded in proving you were right about your desire not manifesting. "I told you so!" you can say. "I told you none of this manifestation clap-trap works!" Your ship never came in because you kept it away with your waves of incessant doubts and negative beliefs. This further entrenched you, and you became even more resistant to trying to manifest anything else again.

As children, we're closer to Source Energy. All things seem possible at a young age. Life is colorful, fun, and full of promise. By the time we hit high school, though, we've been taught thousands of times to expect less color, fun, and promise; and in turn, to expect disappointment. The older we get—and the more disconnected from Source Energy we become—the more the magic of life and our dreams fade; new ideas and inspirations never even make it past the outer parameters of our judgmental minds because we've been sold on the idea that dreams do not come true.

An Unwavering Sense of Belief Is Required to Get What You Want

I wrote earlier that I dislike the connotation of the word *faith*. Perhaps Napoleon Hill did too, which might explain why he came up with his own understanding of the word, which coincides with the integrity of *Think and Grow Rich*:

> FAITH is the head chemist of the mind. When FAITH is blended with the vibration of thought, the subconscious mind instantly picks up the vibration and translates it into its spiritual equivalent, and transmits it to Infinite Intelligence, as in the case of prayer.

This definition requires you to be actively engaged in seeding and maintaining an unwavering sense of *knowing* that your burning desire is on the way. This is the most critical piece to manifesting all the things you truly want in your life. Period. No exceptions! Without this sense of determined faith—this inner knowing—even if you practice the other principles of gaining riches, you will not get results. Faith is an irreplaceable part of the equation.

The way in which I operate my successful businesses is grounded in my *unwavering knowing* that everything will be okay. When I'm facing certain challenges, sure, I might momentarily feel that my life will fall apart. But then I immediately tell myself to just listen for cues from the Universe, follow my intuition, and take inspired action. Then I *let go*, knowing that it will all work out. In fact, everything tends to work out much better than I could have ever planned. It works out every single time!

No matter what you're stressing out about—whether it's money, relationships, career, health, or whatever is consuming you—this same strategy of *just letting go* works. Let go of all negativity surrounding your situation, and just let the chips fall as they may.

I like to use the worst-case-scenario approach at times to help myself let go. I'll say, "What's the worst that can happen?" For my business concerns, my doomsday answer is always: "The entire enterprise will fall apart, and I'll have to close my doors." That leads me to: "Okay, so then I'll get to do something else." I stop trying to control the outcome and *just know* that regardless of what happens, I'll be okay. I trust my innate abilities and acquired skills in whatever endeavor I decide to take on, knowing that everything will always turn out all right. Just *knowing* that everything will be okay is how I overcome fear in all aspects of my life.

It is truly magical—divine, really—that once I'm able to fully let go, I start to get inspiration and guidance from a higher place as to what to do next. I then immediately *act upon* those inspirational thoughts and ideas because I know they're required_action steps that always bring me even more wealth, success, and happiness.

All of this is possible because I *know*: I *know* everything will work out no matter what. I *know* the ideas given to me are from the highest and purest vibrational levels. I *know* that my ideas and inspiration are guiding me to manifest my burning desire.

There's an important issue to discuss if bringing a particular person into your life is your desire: *You cannot force others to do anything against their will.* Anytime you try to change the path of someone else's purpose in life, it's a violation of Universal Law. So, if a desire to attract a particular individual isn't manifesting, make sure you're not encroaching upon this person's will and purpose!

What It Means to Struggle

In the summer of 2017, I took my daughter on a ten-day Disney cruise through the Mediterranean. We started in Barcelona, sailed to the South of France, and traveled all through Italy. Our last Italian stop was Sicily. On the day of departure, heading back to the home port in Spain, our 84,000-ton ship ground to a halt because of a small boat bobbing about in the middle of the sea. It was full of Syrian refugees, many of them children, with nothing more than the shirts on their backs. They looked exhausted, scared, and sunburned, and I'm sure they were starving and thirsty as well.

I saw for myself the *real struggles* that occur in the world instead of just seeing them on the news from the comfort of my couch. That's when I realized that humans' fight for survival is very real. As I peeled back the thick veil of desensitivity that I had allowed into my mind, I felt shocked by the vast disparity between the well-heeled passengers on our gorgeous Disney ship—its bow painted with Sorcerer Mickey and its aft painted with a hilarious Goofy—and this small boat of refugees who just wanted a better life, who were being plucked out one at a time to board the Sicilian coast-guard rescue ship. It made my heart cry that day. And it also made me more aware of how blessed I am.

Those refugees and millions of others are suffering around the world every day. There is suffering happening right now as you read this sentence and as you stay stuck in your own personal beliefs that you have a hard life. If you're able to read and comprehend this book, then you must know that your life isn't that difficult; you simply have unrealized opportunities to improve your life.

You also probably live in a first-world country like the United States. Billions of people living elsewhere could spend a lifetime trying to reach what you were born into and perhaps take for granted. Whining about your difficulties when opportunity is all around you all the time isn't logical. You don't realize it, but you were born spoiled, which has likely made you narrow-minded if you believe that your life is a struggle. If you feel that way, think of those Syrian refugees off the coast of Sicily. Think of being one of *them*. Then take another look at how hard you think you have it.

One Person's Survival Is Another Person's Luxury

Let's go back to this: How can you know that money is coming when you seemingly have no career prospects, no income, and no money in the bank? This is where creativity must come into play.

You must be willing to expand your knowledge base, even just a little bit.

First of all, let's talk about how you managed to make it this far. I'm assuming you've had resources of some kind for food or you wouldn't be alive to read this book. How have you managed to have a roof over your head—a house, apartment, or a tent on the side of the freeway? Regardless of your circumstances, you've been living somewhere, right? Why worry about the future when you've been okay from the beginning up till the present moment?

You might be saying, "Sure, I've been eating and have a roof over my head, but there's a lot more to life than just surviving. So, no, Monica, I'm not okay." You're not okay? Really? And why not? You've been surviving up till this point. Surviving is significant, *very* significant. But you probably think dog-eat-dog survival means still driving your fourteen-year-old Subaru, having to cancel your Netflix account, and making do with an iPhone 6. But that's quite a different view of survival for billions of others, like those Syrian refugees. Or like the guy serving a life sentence for a crime he didn't commit. Or like the lady with stage 4 breast cancer who only has a few months to live. So, be honest: Are you at their survival level?

It's time for you to be deeply appreciative and grateful that you've had the skills, wherewithal, street smarts, and chutzpah to make it this far in life. You can now *know* this to be true because you being here right now *proves* that it's true! So when it comes to manifesting your dreams, just know that it will happen, and leave it at that.

The First Technique:
Think about the Things You Know for Sure

Think about only the things you *know for sure*. You know you've survived to this point. You know you're doing okay right at this moment. (After all, you're not being attacked by a hive of killer bees or hanging from a cliff by your fingernails; so right at this precise moment, consider yourself A-OK!) You know you've eaten today, or will eat soon. You know you have friends and family.

What else do you know for sure, without a doubt? Think about ten of these things, and write them down in a What-I-Know List.

Here are some examples of the things that *I* know for sure:

1. I know I'm okay right at this moment and that I'll always be okay, no matter what.

2. I know that I've eaten today.

3. I know that I'm loved by my friends and family; I know I love and appreciate them.

4. I know that I'm loved by my daughter and that I love her more than anything in this world.

5. I know that I love my furry children—pets, in case you didn't get it—and they love me.

6. I know that I really love to drink tea!

7. I know that I love pineapples from Hawaii, all things pineapple, and I have a cat named Pineapple.

8. I know that I live in a beautiful home with a beautiful pool and have two beautiful luxury cars.

9. I know that this book will be a #1 *New York Times* bestseller.

10. I know that Oprah will read this book, love it, and interview me, bringing massive exposure to this amazing work!

Did you notice what I did on my list? Items 1 through 8 are things I know for sure, and they have already manifested in my life. For items 9 and 10, I am in the "I know" flow, welcoming them to be manifested. How do I know this book will be a #1 *New York Times* bestseller? How do I know that Oprah will read it and interview me? Because this is something I've been visualizing for quite some time, to the point where I've come to believe it so much that I now know it to be a fact, without a single doubt in any fiber of my being. Plus, once I'm in the "I know" flow with my energy vibes raised with flying colors, I can add other things that I have a burning desire for. As an example, I might align myself with the audio version of this book being a bestseller on iTunes, or this work being translated into other languages around the world.

How do you know if something is meant to happen in *your* life? What if you want to be a movie star but have questions such as: *Is this really my path in life? Is this really something I can pull off? Is this part of my destiny?*

While I can't answer that for you, what I *can* say is, if you want it, you can have it. If you desire it, you can attract it. You can become it, and it can become a part of you. It's worth spending extra time doing these tested-and-proven techniques to solidify a deep, unbridled sense of *knowing* that cannot be shaken, even if the worst-case scenarios arise.

Now, if you can't quite get to the place where you know things in your life will happen before they've taken place, just stick to focusing on what you know will make you happy and content right now, even if they're simple things like sipping on a vanilla caramel latte . . . or the anticipation of meeting a friend for dinner and how fun that will be . . . or thinking about the joke you heard the other day that had you in stitches. That is, focus on the things that give you that sense of childlike Christmas-morning excitement and joy. Then, once you're in the Zone, send your *intentions* out to the Universe.

The Second Technique: Say: "I Intend . . ."

Like so many people, I hate New Year's resolutions. I find them to be a drab list of "things to do" that usually never get done, much like that weekend list of chores. It's like an adult version of a letter to Santa Claus: "I want . . . I want . . . I want . . . ," all the while knowing that there's no Kris Kringle or Dasher, Dancer, and Prancer.

If this sounds like you too, *stop writing them altogether*! In fact, chuck any list, even your grocery list, that doesn't work for you, and start an "I intend" list. When you say and write those words, they send out a unique vibrational energy, as if commanding the Universe to part the seas for you and deliver you what you want—stat! *Intend* also feels like a hybrid word between "I want" and "I will get."

So let's put these two powerful words to use and see how they feel to you.

The Run-of-the-Mill Boring List	The "I Intend" List
I want to lose ten pounds in ten weeks.	I INTEND to lose ten pounds in ten weeks.
I want a new car.	I INTEND to manifest a brand-new car.
I need to clean my garage.	I INTEND to clean and organize my garage.
I need a new wardrobe.	I INTEND to get a beautiful new wardrobe.
I really should get a divorce.	I INTEND to free myself from this marriage.
I need to finish this report for work.	I INTEND to write a stellar, informative report.
I want a new laptop.	I INTEND to get an awesome new laptop.
I have to run some errands.	I INTEND to have fun running errands.
I need to find a new job.	I INTEND to create a profitable new career.
I want a new relationship.	I INTEND to manifest a loving partner.

The reason "I intend" is so much more powerful than "I need" or "I want" is because you're coming from a place of love rather than fear. "I intend" empowers you to make things happen. To make your intentions even more powerful, *be specific*—the more specific, the better. For example, using the list above, you can be crystal clear about your intent to make sure you receive what you want from the Universe, as the following list shows:

The Crystal-Clear, Specific I INTEND List
I INTEND to lose ten pounds in ten weeks by adopting a healthy eating plan.
I INTEND to manifest a brand-new car: a fully loaded black Mercedes-Benz AMG S 63 coupe.
I INTEND to clean and organize my garage this weekend while rockin' out to kick-ass tunes.
I INTEND to get a fashionable new wardrobe with designer labels at my favorite clothing store.
I INTEND to free myself from this marriage by meeting with an attorney tomorrow morning.
I INTEND to write a stellar, informative report that will blow everybody at the office away.
I INTEND to get an awesome new laptop, a MacBook Pro with an Intel Core i9 processor.
I INTEND to have fun running errands because I'm going to buy my favorite latte first.
I INTEND to create a profitable new way to make money that I can do from home.
I INTEND to manifest a loving partner who meshes with me in every way possible.

The Third Technique:
Be Grateful for What You Have Right Now

I was doing laundry the other day and felt grateful when I pulled all my clothes out of the dryer and got a whiff of the warm dryer sheet. I had an overwhelming sense of thankfulness for my washer and dryer, my beautiful clothes, and my lovely home. I was also gratified that my laundry was completely done for the week!

I believe that my feelings of deep appreciation are a big part of why I'm continually gifted with more material items, more success, and more happiness. I'm grateful for the orange tree in my backyard. I'm grateful for clean water to bathe in. I'm grateful for the fresh groceries I buy each week. I'm grateful for my sweet and loving pets. I'm grateful for my wonderful daughter who lights up my life in every way. I'm just blessed in every way imaginable, and I honor my blessings every day through my *deep sense of gratitude*. I strongly suggest you do the same—with genuineness, and with no strings attached. Attracting more goodness into your life is a natural result; it is not a quid pro quo that you bargain over.

You might be grumbling, "Easy for you to say. You have tons of money coming in from your thriving businesses to buy all of that great stuff. Must be easy to be 'grateful' for a BMW. I drive a junk car, I live in a three-hundred-square-foot basement apartment under a Chinese restaurant, and I work two jobs—both for minimum wage. My own washer and dryer? Heck, the kitchen sink is my washer, and a string across my apartment is my dryer."

Well, you're focusing on all the negativity. With your thought laser-beamed on low vibes, you just suck in *more* of what you're concentrating on, like a vacuum cleaner. The good news is that just as easily as you created all this lack, you can just as easily create abundance, happiness, health, and bliss.

Read that again: *You can just as easily create abundance, happiness, health, and bliss.*

Just turn your focus dial from a negative channel to a positive channel. Start by thinking about and having feelings of appreciation, satisfaction, and gratitude for all that is good in your life right now.

Let's turn that dial together, my friend!

The Fourth Technique:
Think about Something That Really Makes You Excited

To get yourself in the feeling "mood" for manifestation, you have to bring your vibration up as high as you can crank it, and you have to do it fast. So far, I've revealed that the secret to getting what you want is to connect with Source Energy, which I also refer to as the Zone. Napoleon Hill refers to it as *Infinite Intelligence* or the *ether*. Esther Hicks—as Abraham—refers to it as the *Vortex*. You can call it God, the Universe, Universal Intelligence, God Source, God Consciousness, or the Billy Bob County Fair—whatever you want. What *is* important, though, is that you lift yourself into this vibratory state of blissful exhilaration so you can then tap into a direct connection with Source Energy.

When I'm blue and feel that I can't bring my mood up, I start to think about things that make me really excited. Sometimes I'll play some upbeat music, and even get up and dance around. Getting your body moving to music is a powerful way to get into the Zone. The goal is to disconnect from any thoughts that are bringing you down and focus only on the things that bring you up—*Ecstatic! Pumped! Booyah!*

Once you get into the Zone, you'll feel "buzzy," high, but without drugs or alcohol. You'll feel joyous. You'll feel generous. You'll feel *invincible*. The Zone is where *all things are created*, so put yourself on autopilot, and get there fast and often.

The Fifth Technique:
Think Thoughts *with Feeling* to Create
a *Knowing* Inside You

Below is Napoleon Hill's most significant passage in the original *Think and Grow Rich*:

ALL THOUGHTS WHICH HAVE BEEN EMOTIONALIZED (given feeling) AND MIXED WITH FAITH, begin immediately to translate themselves into their physical equivalent or counterpart.

The emotions, or the "feeling" portion of thoughts, are the factors which give thoughts vitality, life and action. The emotions of Faith, Love, and Sex, when mixed with any thought impulse, give it greater action than any of these emotions can do singly.

Not only thought impulses which have been mixed with FAITH, but those which have been mixed with any of the positive emotions, or any of the negative emotions, may reach, and influence the subconscious mind.

From this statement, you will understand that the subconscious mind will translate into its physical equivalent, a thought impulse of a negative or destructive nature, just as readily as it will act upon thought impulses of a positive or constructive nature. This accounts for the strange phenomenon which so many millions of people experience, referred to as "misfortune," or "bad luck."

There are millions of people who BELIEVE themselves "doomed" to poverty and failure, because of some strange force over which they BELIEVE they have no control. They are the creators of their own "misfortunes," because of this negative BELIEF, which is picked up by the subconscious mind, and translated into its physical equivalent.

This is an appropriate place at which to suggest again that you may benefit, by passing on to your subconscious mind, any DESIRE which you wish translated into its physical, or monetary equivalent, in the state of expectancy or BELIEF that the transmutation will actually take place. Your BELIEF, or FAITH, is the element which determines the action of your subconscious mind. There is nothing to hinder you from "deceiving" your subconscious mind when giving it instructions through autosuggestion.

To make this "deceit" more realistic, conduct yourself just as you would, if you were ALREADY IN POSSESSION OF THE MATERIALS THING WHICH YOU ARE DEMANDING, when you call upon your subconscious mind.

The subconscious mind will transmute into its physical equivalent, by the most direct and practical media available, any order which is given to it in a state of BELIEF, or FAITH that the order will be carried out.

Surely, enough has been stated to give a starting point from which one may, through experiment and practice, acquire the ability to mix FAITH with any order given to the subconscious mind. Perfection will come through practice. It cannot come by merely reading instructions.

The Sixth Technique: Feel a Deep Sense of Love

Each and every morning, there's this thing I do with my dog, Sally. Usually the morning hour is a little chilly—whether it's summer or winter—based on the consistent seventy-degree temperature I keep in my bedroom most of the time. My dog is about fourteen pounds, and she loves blankets and being cuddled. So, right as I crack open my eyes while waking from my slumber, I'll pat my pillow twice, and my little Sally will leap into a small indent between my pillow and my chest. She'll burrow down into this crack as I pull a blanket over her. This is what I call *ultimate snuggles*, and I do it every morning when I'm home.

Just thinking about this brightens my mood. Thinking of Sally's little face and her big, brown doe eyes makes me feel a deep sense of unconditional love that I really don't get anywhere else. This feeling of love inside of me that I get from ultimate snuggles in the morning puts me on the trajectory of being in a great state of high-flying vibes as I start my day.

If you don't have a pet, I recommend that you adopt one. Pets offer unconditional love in a way that humans don't. Dogs and cats can also help lower your blood pressure and stress levels when they're in your presence, especially when you're interacting with them in some way, such as petting them or playing with them. Even *thinking* about your pet can put you in a warm and fuzzy fun-loving mood.

This is a picture of Sally. Don't you just want to melt with love when you look at that little face?

The Seventh Technique:
Use Your First Waking Moments to Set Up Your Day

I believe it's critical to have some kind of a positive subliminal or guided-meditation regimen each night before falling asleep. This allows you to abolish all negativity you've experienced during the day while laying an important positive imprint onto your mind as you drift away into sleep.

As you wake up in the morning, instead of beginning the thought process of rehashing the negatives of the prior day (or week), use those magical minutes to think about what your burning desire is. Feel your burning desire as though it's manifesting in your life right now. This is, hands down, the most powerful moment of your day to practice the art of deliberate manifestation. Why squander this time by thinking about what happened yesterday, or by obsessing over the drab list of chores you have to do today? Instead, harness that magical moment to manifest your desires at an even faster speed than you ever thought possible!

Just recently I woke up from a deep sleep and was still feeling the magic of my dream that morning. I was telling myself, "Of course all of these things are possible! *Everything* is possible!" But then as my body woke up a little more, I started thinking about the "realities" of my life as if the quarks, molecules, and atoms were scurrying around me to create my current perception, much like feeling a layer of concrete quickly drying around my entire body. I thought to myself, *This is interesting. Only a moment ago, this other world was possible because I wholly believed it. Now my brain has sold me on this other "reality," so the magical world disappeared while I felt this other reality lock in around me. But what if I just stayed in that magical morning state longer, while lacing in my burning desire? Would the manifestation process occur much faster?*

I found out that I *can* manifest things much faster by using this morning magical period, right before the brain fully wakes up and is able to throw water on the fire with the "logic" and "impossibility" of the conscious mind. Try it. You'll be pleasantly surprised by the results. Tomorrow morning, before jumping out of bed to start your day, take about five minutes to lie there and think about your deepest desires. Imagine what it'll be like when they manifest. *Feel* what it'll be like when they become a part of your life. The cool thing about doing this the moment you wake up is that your logical mind hasn't had a chance to fully awaken to put a damper on what your new reality can be. You essentially race ahead of your fully awakened conscious mind by visualizing and feeling the manifestation of your desire before your brain has a chance to talk you out of it. It's really quite powerful and can change your life in no time at all if you do this each and every day.

The Eighth Technique:
Find Your Life "Snapshot," and Have One
Everywhere You Look

I have a snapshot of what I want my life to look like. Yes, it's one single snapshot that represents everything I want to become. I have it everywhere. It's in my home office, my work office, my master bathroom, my closet, my manifestation book, my wallet, and everywhere else you can think of. Here's what it looks like:

I have so many of these pictures everywhere that it drives my daughter crazy. What it represents is what I want my future to look like. It represents my new life. Having these pictures everywhere helps to train my subconscious mind to believe that this new life is possible for me since the mind responds much more powerfully to pictures than to words.

What does this future snapshot represent to me? It is how I envision a life as a successful writer, writing on the beach in paradise with a refreshing coconut drink on hand. I can live the life I want, writing wherever I choose, and living anywhere in the world

I'd like to live. It represents me writing about things I'm most passionate about that can help improve people's lives in some way. This is my true purpose or my chief aim in life. What is *your* true purpose in life? What is your chief aim? Most important, what is your burning desire? What single snapshot best depicts what you want out of your life right now?

If It's All about Money, It's Pretty Lonely at the Top

I spoke at an event recently and was asked the most interesting and profound question I've ever gotten, and I've spoken to thousands of people over the years. A young millennial woman asked, "I found it interesting when you said that you went into a deep depression after you made all this money and you hit that peak, asking yourself, 'Is this it?' How do you avoid that—I mean, going into a depression like that?"

What she was referring to was a story I'd spoken of at past events, where, after I explained that upon making millions of dollars, I hit a "peak" and then slid into a devastating depression for many months afterward. I don't know what I expected to feel after making all that money. Maybe I felt that trumpet players would announce my arrival while confetti and balloons flew around the room. Maybe I thought I'd feel regal, as if a red carpet would be rolled out while being offered a golden key to some faraway kingdom. Truth is, I never thought about it, but if I had, I'm sure depression would not have even crossed my mind. Yes, I had everything—the house, the cars, the status, the success—and yet I'd never felt emptier and more insignificant in my entire life. It took me a while to find my way back, which was interesting in itself because it was the same path that had led to my success in the first place.

My advice for not getting into this type of rut yourself is: *Always be in meaningful service to others. As long as you're living a life of service, you'll never feel depressed or insignificant because your life becomes about serving others and not just about serving yourself.*

Your life becomes bigger than just being about you. Service is any way you can help make other people's lives better. As long as you do so in a meaningful way, your life will have purpose and significance.

⬥═══⬥

Years ago I was diagnosed with bipolar disorder. It turns out that many successful people have psychological or brain ailments, including depressive tendencies. At times it seems like it's almost a requirement to be neurotic enough to have grandiose ideas of near-impossible magnitude, to be "out there" taking certain risks, and to have the chutzpah to pull it off. But some people simply aren't wired that way. They're "normal," which might have something to do with why those with this personality type struggle more to reach the heights of their potential.

Maybe for you, instead of thinking that your success is all about making money or finding the partner of your dreams or manifesting possessions, make it about doing something you're utterly passionate about that can help a lot of other people in the process.

Motivational speaker Zig Ziglar said it best: "You can have everything in life that you want, if you just help other people get what they want."

Get into the "Know"

Feeling passionate about some kind of meaningful service will align you with Source Energy and point the way to your bliss. If you're not aligned, it will be impossible for you to reach the high vibrational alignment that will allow you to find yourself in the first place. Getting what you want in life requires a lot of energy from a higher vibrational power, which in a practical sense means that you need to access it almost constantly. If you don't have the ability or desire to stay tapped in or "plugged" in to this Source Energy, you probably don't want whatever it is you desire badly enough. If you're forcing yourself to do something for the money or because you believe you have to live up to societal expectations, you'll never, ever be able to get into and stay in the required state of "knowing" enough.

The easiest way to get in the "know" is to be of meaningful service to others and live out your passions—despite what anyone else thinks—because you'll need that rocket-booster blast from your direct alignment with Source Energy. To serve is powerful and noble. If you want some help in clarifying your vision, ask yourself the following questions:

- How can I serve?

- What product or service can I offer to the world that will benefit many people?

- What product or service can I provide and/or sell that will change people's lives or make them happy or help them achieve their own dreams?

Your vision can be as simple as offering a product that helps people clean their clothes (for example, a biodegradable detergent) or as complex as helping people manage their chronic pain (cognitive behavioral therapy, or CBT). When you focus on serving others, you gain fulfillment and also a path to unlimited financial wealth.

One of the most frustrating things for me when I train people about investments or starting a business is when they ask me to just cut to the chase and tell them how to get rich *now*. They don't have any real interest in doing the actual "thing" that I teach. It wouldn't matter if I hand-delivered a comprehensive, step-by-step wealth-building plan for them based on the principles I believe in; they'd quickly find themselves up against a brick wall because they didn't believe in the principles of living in the Zone. In fact, nobody can become successful implementing somebody else's wealth plan if they don't believe in it themselves. All individuals must create their *own* paths based on what their inner guidance tells them. Yes, you can start with a blueprint from someone else, which is what I offer, but eventually you'll have to break the mold and sculpt your own life story, which is tailor-made for *you*. Simply follow your passion—there's *always* a way to make a lot of money if you do just that!

Tap into What Lights Your Fire Right Now

Be patient as you wait for inspiration as to how to follow your passion and thrive while doing so. Remember that the joy is in the journey and not just in the destination. Trust that the next chapter in your life experience will reveal itself as you accept what feels good to you and as ideas and inspirational thoughts are given to you from a higher level. When those lofty thoughts arrive, keep taking action on them, knowing that the next path on your journey will always be revealed to you until you get where you ultimately wish to be.

Chapter Four

THE THIRD STEP TOWARD RICHES: AUTO-SUGGESTION, VISUALIZATION, AND AFFIRMATIONS

....

Creative visualization is magic in the truest and highest meaning of the word.

—SHAKTI GAWAIN

....

A number of years ago, there was an experiment conducted by Masaru Emoto, a Japanese doctor of alternative medicine. In one of his books, *The Hidden Messages in Water,* he provided documented proof that thoughts and feelings *do affect physical reality*—namely, water, in the case of his laboratory experiments. Through Emoto's research, he was able to see a "change in expression" when water was "spoken" to depending on whether the words—and intentions behind the words—were positive or negative. For example, saying, "You make me sick" showed the water looking putrid and sickly with a greenish-brown hue to it. On the flip side, saying "love and gratitude" resulted in the water appearing as glorious, white, crystallized snowflake-like molecules.

Through many years of analysis and thousands of experiments using high-powered microscopes coupled with high-speed photography, Emoto was able to offer scientific evidence that thoughts, attitudes, and emotions are forces that deeply impact the environment, the earth, the world around us, and our personal health. Thinking and saying things that are negative *will result in negative results*. Thinking and saying things that are positive *will result in positive results*.

The human body is approximately 60 percent water; the brain is about 73 percent water. When we talk to ourselves with sweet encouragement, as water-based creatures it seems we would respond positively in the same way the water molecules did in Emoto's experiments. It follows, then, that when we tell ourselves unpleasant things, we would respond negatively. I use the word *seems*, but in fact it is more than that: I *know* this is true.

In the past, I've viewed daily positive affirmations as a ridiculously Pollyannaish attempt to improve one's life. But after performing some experiments on myself by doing what I call "gentle self-talk," I'm now convinced that using affirmations correctly and consistently can change lives.

When I was diagnosed with bipolar disorder in a mild form called cyclothymia, I never bought into this label. First of all, I don't believe in labels. Also, I believe that everyone has bouts of depression, sadness, and self-doubt that don't rise to the level of a clinical diagnosis.

However, the awareness that my condition gave me has been that I'm now painfully aware of the barrage of disparaging thoughts I sometimes fire at myself when settling into a low vibratory state. It has also brought about major changes in my diet—namely, ditching complex carbohydrates such as bread and pasta—because certain foods fuel depressive tailspins. The negative thoughts and poor diet lowered my vibrations even more, stripping away any faith and belief that I could get what I want in life.

What you say in your head or out loud—to yourself and to others—makes a *huge* difference. What you focus on, what you watch on television, what you listen to, what you read, and what you absorb—consciously and subconsciously—dramatically effects every aspect of how you feel, think, and believe. This is beyond the land of Pollyanna. If you affirm and visualize in the right way—consistently—it can truly change your life and open magical doors.

What Does "Auto-Suggestion" Really Mean?

To affirm or suggest something to yourself is what Napoleon Hill calls *auto-suggestion*, which is the *Think and Grow Rich* principle that is most widely misunderstood. So, what does auto-suggestion *really* mean, and most important, how do you properly implement it for maximum results? Let's start with some of Hill's views:

> NO THOUGHT, whether it be negative or positive, CAN ENTER THE SUBCONSCIOUS MIND <u>WITHOUT</u> THE AID OF THE PRINCIPLE OF AUTO-SUGGESTION, with the exception of thoughts picked up from the ether.
>
> Nature has so built man that he has ABSOLUTE CONTROL over the material which reaches his subconscious mind, through his five senses, although this is not meant to be constructed as a statement that man always EXERCISES this control. In the great majority of instances, he does NOT exercise it, which explains why so many people go through life in poverty.

Living in this moment in time, I believe there has never been any period before when people have been subjected to so much confusion, distraction, propaganda, disconnection, despondency, hopelessness, and doubt. With millions of things flying at us all the time—particularly since we've given over our physical, mental, and emotional attention to technological devices—we're even more sensitive to the worst possible conscious and subconscious programming in human history. The solution is that we must take *active control* of what we tell and sell ourselves. Otherwise we will feel adrift, unable to steer in the direction of our dreams.

As Catherine Ponder wrote in her book *The Prosperity Secret of the Ages*, "When you rule your mind, you rule your world. When you choose your thoughts, you choose results."

How to Seize Instant Control Over Your Mind

Before you can even begin to control your mind on a moment-to-moment basis, you must first *become aware* and then *actively identify* the corrupt information you're voluntarily consuming.

Yes, it's true: you are *voluntarily* allowing your smartphones, tablets, social media accounts, mainstream media reports, and every bit of information you take in to influence you . . . and in many cases, to manipulate you. For you to take control of your mind, you *must immediately stop* the influx of the contaminated material being dumped into your brain moment by moment, day in and day out.

This means being willing to completely and fully disconnect from it. I recommend that you remove all electronics including laptops, tablets, TVs, and smartphones from your bedroom at night. Comprehensive studies on the biological damage these devices cause the brain and body by altering energy fields have not yet been completed; however, the initial results are not pretty. The emerging scientific consensus is that addiction to technology affects the brain in the same ways that substance abuse does.

If you're unwilling to disconnect from and implement strict control over the use of what is directly and indirectly polluting your mind, you will not be able to get what you desire. Simply stopping the inflow of harmful thoughts, ideas, and feelings, in and of itself, has the potential to completely change your life! When the cesspool of information stops flowing into your mind, you'll be able to see things clearly, perhaps for the first time in many years. You'll get back your true identity—apart from news broadcasts, social media feeds, game apps, and talk-radio discussions—and with that, your own thoughts, ideas, dreams, and mental and emotional processes.

It will take some time to disconnect from these mind contaminants, but once you get past the "withdrawal," your brain will have formed new habits that will lead to a newfound freedom. Your identity will be restored in whole—that is, you will *reclaim your power* as it was *originally intended to be*, allowing you to then tap into what you want rather than what society has made you believe you should have, think, or feel.

I've personally noticed an increased number of higher-echelon people getting rid of their brain-rotting "smart" phones and opting for more old-fashioned (yet expensive) "flip phones" that do not have the brainwave-altering and addictive traits, since these high-net-worth individuals value their time and productivity.

Change the Inflow of Thoughts and Feelings from Negative to Positive

The next step to gaining control of your mind is to put good thoughts into that head of yours, starting with self-encouragement and self-praise for the things you love about yourself.

I recommend starting with a new declaration of who you are. My daughter taught me this technique. She was a toddler, barely talking, when she declared: "I am an artist." She did not say she was an "aspiring" artist or that she'd *be* an artist one day. Straight-up, from toddler to the young woman she is today, she's been consistent: "I *am* an artist."

When she was nine years old, I remember her asking for help with an English assignment. I have a graduate degree in writing, so she always hits me up for answers on anything related to spelling, sentence structure, storylines, character dialogue, and so on. One day she asked me one of these questions, but because I was in the middle of something else, I didn't quite grasp it. Feeling frustrated, I said, "I just don't know right now." She quickly responded, "How can you *not* know? You're a writer."

Once she insisted that I was a writer, I stopped what I was doing and thought for a minute, but what came out of my mouth wasn't my proudest moment: "I'm not really a writer . . . not yet. I write books and courses for my business, but that's not like being a *real* writer like the kind you're thinking of." I figured she was thinking of J. K. Rowling or Roald Dahl—*professional* writers, a group I felt I wasn't a part of.

She looked at me, confused by my response. Suddenly I felt awash with shame in affirming my feelings of inferiority to a young girl who I was, and still am, guiding to become a power-house in her own right. From that day forward, I have always declared: "I *am* a writer."

To embark on your journey to being the person you want to become, you must declare that your aim is a reality *right now*. If you want to own a successful business, start with a present-tense statement such as "I am a successful business owner." To really make this work, you must get into a *feeling state* through which you "know" you're already a successful business owner, even if your current position is sweeping floors for minimum wage.

To reach this "knowing" connection between your conscious and subconscious mind—between sweeping floors and running your own successful business—you will likely have to create "bridge" affirmations such as: "This is a temporary point in my life, and it's just a matter of time before I have my own hugely successful business. Everybody has to start somewhere, and this is my place to gather the tools I need. I know I am attracting the right opportunities right now that lead to my success." Without a bridge, you might find yourself swirling in a whirlpool of negative emotions and thoughts, comparing where you hope to be with where you are now. *Honor* where you are *right now*.

Most recently I changed some of the negative thinking I've had for too many years. I'd always referred to myself, somewhat disparagingly, as a "single mom." I felt a sense of dread, disap-pointment, hurt, and anger over this aspect of my life. But the truth is, I'm a freaking awesome mom in all that I've been able to do for my daughter. So when I decided to change "single mom" to "super mom," I gained great power, confidence, and self-worth!

Create a Positive Money Consciousness with Affirmations and Feelings

If you don't have a *money consciousness*, you will not be rich. If you don't have a *health consciousness*, you will not be healthy.

If you don't have a *fitness consciousness*, you will not be fit. If you don't have a *love consciousness*, you will not be filled with love. And if you don't have a *happiness consciousness*, you will not be happy.

So, what *is* a consciousness, and how do you develop one?

The conscious mind is what you're aware of. For example, you're aware that you're reading this book right now. You understand what you think, feel, say, sense, and more.

The subconscious mind is what you're *not* aware of. You may have heard the word *bloatware*. Tech-repair guys use it all the time. It means that your computer has a lot of useless, space-sucking software running in the background, slowing down its processing. Well, when your subconscious mind lets in too many bad things, allowing them to imprint themselves on your brain, it becomes like bloatware clogging up your life. However, positive things that get imprinted in your subconscious mind help you—for example, automatically looking both ways before crossing a busy street. Napoleon Hill offered more insights in *Think and Grow Rich*:

> Here is a most significant fact—the subconscious mind takes any orders given it in a spirit of absolute FAITH, and acts upon those orders, although the orders often have to be presented over and over again, through repetition, before they are interpreted by the subconscious mind. Following the preceding statement, consider the possibility of playing a perfectly legitimate "trick" on your subconscious mind, by making it believe, *because you believe it*, that you must have the amount of money you are visualizing, that this money is already awaiting your claim, that the subconscious mind MUST hand over to you practical plans for acquiring the money which is yours.

When I was really young, we used to get the Sears & Roebuck catalog at our home at least once a year. If you're around my age or older, you may remember how the catalog was thicker in size than most major metropolitan phonebooks. I'd haul it to my room and circle all the things I wanted with a black marker. I was too young at that time to think, *My parents are too broke to ever buy me any of this.* I was still a dreamer, a believer that all things were possible.

That all changed one year when my mother walked in as I was circling a bunch of stuff I wanted, and said, "I used to do that, too, when I was a kid." Apparently my subconscious mind did a quick scan of her body language and the tone of her voice, and inferred that she meant: *I used to be a pitiful dreamer, too, and look how that turned out for me. Life will probably turn out to be the same for you.*

I remember slowly putting down the marker and closing the catalog. My subconscious mind in that moment imprinted: *You're just a dreamer who will never get the things you want in the catalog. So why bother dreaming at all anymore? Stop circling the things that you're not going to get anyway. What a waste of time!* I never circled anything in those catalogs ever again.

Hopefully you picked up on the fact that my mother didn't actually *say* those words. All she said was, "I used to do that, too, when I was a kid." But my subconscious mind came up with its own interpretation. I'm sure my mom didn't mean to come across that way, but she certainly did, at least to me.

That, my friend, is how you can destroy the confidence, dreams, and spirits of others—from children to adults. So not only do you have to take great care in watching what you say, but also *how you say it.* By cleansing your subconscious mind of the negative beliefs you've given a home to, you can greatly reduce the chance of hurting others.

Get Started Right Now!

At this time in your life, you may find yourself struggling with finances, in part because you didn't grow up in a family with a lot of money, Or, you may be struggling with relationships because you didn't grow up in a family with a lot of love. This means you have some damage inside that I'm going to show you how to abolish.

I use a particular exercise to help people find personal breakthroughs to move their lives forward. It involves thinking about your first childhood moment when you felt insignificant or not good enough. I'll give you an example from my own life. I remember a time when I was maybe five years old. My family was on a short road trip, probably from Chicago to Michigan or Wisconsin—those were the kinds of occasional day trips we took. We'd stopped at a small country store that had brown wicker baskets with oversize lollipops in them. The top basket was perfect—filled with huge, spectacular lollipops brimming with brilliant blues, reds, oranges, and yellows. I'd never seen anything like it. I immediately got busy picking out my favorites that I couldn't wait to call mine.

But my mother scolded me to put the lollipops back. She gestured to a bottom basket that I hadn't even noticed. It was full of broken candy wrapped in cheap sandwich bags with reduced prices scribbled on it in black marker. She told me to choose a lollipop from one of the broken bags. I remember starting to cry and her having none of it: I'd either choose from one of the broken bags or I'd get nothing at all. I also remember feeling that a little bit of my spirit broke in that moment.

I hadn't recalled that incident until doing this exercise. It was buried so deeply in my subconscious mind, yet it had affected everything I did, everything I thought of myself, and everything I felt I could do in my life. Once I was able to recognize this emotional scar for what it was, I was able to understand the *whys* behind it, which then allowed me to let it go.

Here are the *whys* I discovered:

1. My mom was in her twenties at the time. She was a high school dropout and didn't understand child psychology, nor was she aware of how her actions would affect me throughout my entire life.

2. My parents lived hand-to-mouth. They didn't understand money, business, credit, or how to function in the real world of economics; nobody had taught them anything

about those things up to that point, and they never tried to learn on their own.

3. I subconsciously allowed my five-year-old self who didn't get the candy she wanted to dictate my self-worth well into my adulthood.

It's like a metaphor with you steering your ship through murky waters. But unbeknownst to you, your rudder is completely disengaged, and there's another steering wheel and rudder determining your course. As you look out on the horizon, you say, "I really want to head in that direction," but your ship is sailing elsewhere. You may chalk it up to the weather (your environment, the economy, and so on), or maybe it's just a fluke (your genetics, your luck, and the like). But until you understand that you have self-defeating, subconscious beliefs steering your ship—and then correct them—they'll continue to send you off course.

In order to pinpoint *your* emotional scars, first think back to one or two childhood or adolescent incidents that have deeply affected you, which your subconscious mind keeps using to hold you back—for example, by filling your head with thoughts about why you don't deserve success or love.

These "stem" memories hold you back in another way too: Once your subconscious mind gets a grip, it will only collect information to support its belief, no matter how nonsensical. It will toss away any other evidence—even verifiable facts. For example, with my lollipop incident, from that point forward and well into my adult life, my subconscious mind only collected and held on to information that supported my personal belief that I was worth *less* than others while *discarding* any evidence showing the opposite, including the verifiable fact that my bank account was quite healthy.

Just about everyone has feelings of unworthiness at times. If you're unable to uncover and resolve these emotions, I recommend placing yourself in a safe environment, such as a healing retreat or a professional therapist's office, to help you pull this "stem" to the surface and come to terms with it. Until you do, it will continue to wreak havoc in your life.

Identify the Stem Incident, and Then Reverse the Damage

Let's talk about how to make this new mind-set a permanent change in your life. The easiest solution is: you have to do the work. The good news is that it can be a fun process! Below is how Napoleon Hill described an element of this important work in *Think and Grow Rich*:

> Remember, therefore, when reading aloud the statement of your desire (through which you are endeavoring to develop a 'money consciousness'), that the mere reading of the words is of NO CONSEQUENCE—UNLESS you **mix emotion, or feeling with your words.** If you repeat a million times the famous Emil Coué formula, "Day by day, in every way, I am getting better and better," without mixing emotion and FAITH with your words, you will experience no desirable results. **Your subconscious mind recognizes and acts upon ONLY thoughts which have been well-mixed with emotion or feeling.**
>
> This is a fact of such importance as to warrant repetition in practically every chapter, because the lack of understanding of this is the main reason the majority of people who try to apply the principle of auto-suggestion get no desirable results.
>
> Plain, unemotional words do not influence the subconscious mind. You will get no appreciable results until you learn to reach your subconscious mind with thoughts, or spoken words which have been well emotionalized with BELIEF.

I have another suggestion that can make this process easier: Listen to only uplifting music and, even better, listen to positive-thinking audio books. Do so when you're driving, cleaning your home, working out, or just relaxing on the couch. This, in and of itself, regardless of the uplifting content, can change your life. After all, good in, good out. Junk in, junk out. Not only can negative lyrics about killing people and dealing drugs alter how your subconscious mind processes thoughts, they can also lower your vibratory output, which, as we've discussed, attracts lower-energy conditions such as being broke.

Also, at night, when your subconscious mind is more susceptible to messages of positive thinking, it's best to shut off negative news like the latest murder mystery on *48 Hours* or details about the terrorist attack that killed hundreds of people, and instead, relax into some guided meditations and subliminal audios as you drift off to sleep. Yes, those "old school" tracks really do work, since they're able to leave positive imprints on your subconscious mind that you can take throughout the night and into a new day.

Most evenings at bedtime, my mind is like Grand Central Station, with thoughts moving in and out of the terminal like Amtrak at rush hour. A guided meditation helps me quiet myself while offering positive messages and suggestions to "reset" my thinking from negative to positive as my brain waves slow down for sleep. I've even created my own audio recordings. When I listen to them each night, not only does my life continue to change in miraculous ways, but I stay in the Zone more, and feel fantastic as a result.

I'll explain some of the neuroscience behind this phenomenon, which is not only interesting but will give you a visual image of what's going on with your brain (see the chart that follows for an explanation of the various levels). During waking hours, your brain will ordinarily function at the beta cognitive level. But if you're super sharp, focused, and performing at your peak, it will be functioning at the gamma level. However, most people rarely, if ever, reach this level.

When you're beginning to relax for the night, your brain will slip down into the alpha level. You're really open to suggestions at this point, whether through a guided meditation or hypnosis. This is also a great time to introduce creative visualizations and personal affirmations to attract your burning desire.

As you go deeper, your brain will move into the theta level. This is where you can tap into your intuition through meditation. When I reach this level, I begin remembering the dreams I had during the night. I begin remembering because my brain-wave activity has slowed down to a level that allows it.

The delta level is really deep. The body needs it to heal, refresh, and gain spiritual alignment.

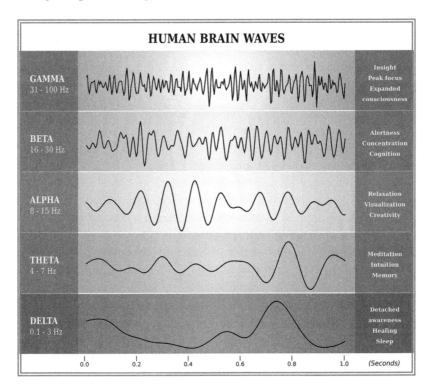

Imagine what a master creator you'd be if you spent every single night before slipping off to sleep envisioning your burning desire. Even more powerful, imagine if you immersed yourself in *feeling* those desires by visualizing what you want to manifest. And to top that, what if you continued on with this feeling state the moment you woke in the morning, staying in it for at least five minutes? You would, indeed, attract everything you ever wanted.

I was able to manifest a move to California when I was only twelve years old, doing exactly what I've outlined above. I visualized what I wanted; I felt what I wanted. It was as if my heart would burst with joy upon its manifestation, and my solar plexus—the emotional center in the stomach area—would expand with light emanating out into the Universe. This is the key to getting everything you want. Imagine that!

So now you're ready to use the power of auto-suggestion to completely transform your life. Here are some instructions from Napoleon Hill from *Think and Grow Rich*, with a few of my own additions noted in brackets:

> The instructions given in connection with the six steps in the second chapter will now be summarized, and blended with the principles covered by this chapter, as follows:
>
> First. Go into some quiet spot [preferably in bed at night] where you will not be disturbed or interrupted, close your eyes, and repeat aloud [so you may hear your own words] the written statement of the amount of money [or whatever you desire] you intend to accumulate or manifest, the time limit for its accumulation, and a description of the service or merchandise you intend to give in return for the money. As you carry out these instructions, SEE YOURSELF ALREADY IN POSSESSION OF THE MONEY.
>
> For example: Suppose that you intend to accumulate $1,000,000 by the first of January, five years from now, that you intend to give personal services [or sell something] in return for the money, in the capacity of a salesman [or saleswoman]. Your written statement of your purpose should be similar to the following:
>
> By the first day of January, [20___], I will have in my bank account $1,000,000, which will come to me in various amounts from time to time during the interim.
>
> In return for this money I will give the most efficient service [or sale of a specific product] of which I am capable, rendering the fullest possible quantity, and the best possible quality of service in the capacity of salesman [or saleswoman] of ___. [Describe the service or merchandise you intend to sell.]

I believe that I will have this money in my bank account. My faith is so strong that I can now see this money before my eyes. I can touch it with my hands. It is now awaiting transfer to me at the time, and in the proportion that I deliver the service I intend to render in return for it. I am wide open to a plan by which to accumulate this money, and I will follow that plan, when it is received from the higher sources.

Second. Repeat this program night and morning until you can see [in your imagination] the money [or other thing] you intend to accumulate or manifest.

Third. Place a written copy for your statement when you can see it night and morning, and read it just before going to bed, and upon waking up in the morning until it has been memorized.

Remember, as you carry out these instructions, that you are applying the principle of auto-suggestion, for the purpose of giving orders to your subconscious mind. Remember, also, that your subconscious mind will act ONLY upon instructions which are emotionalized, and handed over to it with "feeling." FAITH is the strongest, and most productive of the emotions. Follow the instructions given in the chapter on FAITH.

Feeling the emanating ball of energy from your solar plexus pulsating through your entire body and pushing its way outward into the Universe *while you are visualizing what you want* is mastery of the principles of success! Napoleon Hill, in *Think and Grow Rich*, was crystal clear about the importance of each of these steps:

After you have read the entire book, come back to this chapter, and follow in spirit, and in action, this instruction:

READ THE ENTIRE CHAPTER ALOUD ONCE EVERY NIGHT, UNTIL YOU BECOME THOROUGHLY CONVINCED THAT THE PRINCIPLE OF AUTO-SUGGESTION IS SOUND, THAT IT WILL ACCOMPLISH FOR YOU ALL THAT HAS BEEN CLAIMED FOR IT. AS YOU READ, <u>UNDERSCORE WITH A PENCIL</u> EVERY SENTENCE WHICH IMPRESSES YOU FAVORABLY.

Follow the foregoing instruction to the letter, and it will open the way for a complete understanding and mastery of the principles of success.

Chapter Five

THE FOURTH STEP TOWARD RICHES: SPECIALIZED KNOWLEDGE FOR BIG BUCKS

....

Knowledge isn't power until it is applied.

—DALE CARNEGIE

....

I didn't officially drop out of high school, but I did stop going to classes when I was just a hair under sixteen. I wanted to *get* out without *dropping* out—that was a pretty firm intention of mine. To you it may just sound like semantics, but for me it was much deeper. I hated high school, yet I didn't want to be like my parents, both high school dropouts and both with nothing but a trail of failures that I attributed to not having completed their formal education.

While leaving gym class one day, I overhead two girls talking about something called the CHSPE. My ears perked up, as the idea of inspiration flowed toward me. One of the girls was saying how she was going to take this exam when she turned sixteen. At that time, I had already explored the possibility of taking the GED exam but wasn't anywhere near the required age of eighteen. I wondered: *What is this CHSPE thing?* I had never heard of it before. *Is this the solution to my desire to leave high school early?*

This was back in 1989 when there was no internet to quickly look things up. So I began my research by poking around the school counselor's office and quickly found out that the acronym CHSPE stood for the California High School Proficiency Exam. To take it, you had to be sixteen years old and/or be academically enrolled in at least the tenth grade for one year. My heart sank for a second: I didn't fit either requirement. But a second later my heart rose: I'd found a loophole:

> "He or she will complete one academic year of enrollment in grade ten at the end of the semester during which the CHSPE regular administration (spring or fall) will be conducted."

Although I was still fifteen, I was permitted to register for the spring exam during my final semester as a sophomore. I bought a study guidebook, crammed night and day, and passed the test with flying colors the first time out. Some weeks later I received my CHSPE certification. I graduated high school early. Even back then I'd had my eye on entrepreneurship, but I enrolled in college anyway because I believed that was the ticket to my dreams. But I was mistaken and quickly found out during my very first college course that college was not for me: the professor teaching the subject of entrepreneurship admitted to having never owned a business himself, so I felt duped.

Many years later I finished both my undergraduate and graduate degrees. I realize now that I did this to: (a) not be like my parents in any way; (b) never have to engage in an argument with my daughter if she balked at getting a college education; and (c) to prove my worth. In hindsight, getting those two degrees helped relieve the burden of my subconscious desire to prove to the world and myself that I was *worthy*, and not the five-year-old girl back in that Midwest general store who could only get the broken lollipops because her parents were poor high school dropouts.

But those degrees also hindered my ability to think creatively, profitably, and limitlessly. If you have a degree, most likely the knowledge you've been taught is the run-of-the-mill clap-trap that college institutions spit out to almost every student, offering nothing more than a "knowledge commodity" that won't help you generate real money in an ever-changing economic marketplace. Napoleon Hill had an understanding of this back in 1937 when *Think and Grow Rich* was first published:

> There are two kinds of knowledge. One is general, the other is specialized. General knowledge, no matter how great the quantity or variety it may be, is of but little use in the accumulation of money. The faculties of the great universities possess, in the aggregate, practically every form of general knowledge known to civilization. Most of the professors have but little or no money. They specialize on teaching knowledge, but they do not specialize on the organization, or the use of knowledge.
>
> KNOWLEDGE will not attract money, unless it is organized, and intelligently directed, through practical PLANS OF ACTION, to the DEFINITE END of accumulation of money. Lack of understanding of this fact has been the source of confusion to millions of people who falsely believe that "knowledge is power." It is nothing of the sort! Knowledge is potential power. It becomes power only when, and if, it is organized into definite plans of action, and directed to a definite end.

Do you know how to do an advanced algebraic formula? Yes? Great! Except the likelihood that somebody will pay you millions of dollars a year for your math skills is, well, mathematically improbable. This is why many self-made billionaires like Bill Gates, Michael Dell, Steve Jobs, Mark Zuckerberg, and others are high school or college dropouts. They dropped out of the think-like-everybody-else box that the school system stuffs students into so they could instead expand their wings with their larger creative visions and ideas. Of course, I'm not advocating becoming a dropout, especially if you're in school right now. Rather, I'm simply offering a bit of advice about what it takes to reach your dreams. Much of it will involve *thinking big* and *thinking outside the box* despite what others around you may recommend.

What Gates, Dell, Jobs, and the others also show is that getting an education doesn't have to mean getting it from someone else or from an accredited institution. The word *educate* is derived from the Latin word *educo*, meaning to "educe, to draw out, or to develop from within."

Structured and organized education can strip away your ability to think outside the box and receive creative thoughts of inspiration. It can discourage you from spreading your wings to manifest big dreams. Many professors and educators themselves are stuck in their own limiting boxes of their own creation. With their own prejudices and biases, they may consciously "teach" a class while subconsciously dissuading you from achieving your dreams.

The Universe Cannot Mail You a Check from the Clouds

Here are the ABCs of how our economic system works. You put out energy in the form of a product or service. People will then pay you for that energy in the form of currency, which you can use to buy food, clothing, shelter, and other things you need and want. Those are the "rules."

Stuart Wilde said it best when he wrote in his book *The Little Money Bible*: "To make money, you must deliver your energy in some form, to satisfy a demand that is out there. And if what you are selling is energy, charisma, and enthusiasm, there is no competition because most others are selling things that are lifeless, loveless, and dull."

What this means is when you put out *any* kind of product or service, it's best that it be something you're truly passionate about. That way you'll be coming from a high vibrational place of enthusiasm and excitement, which is a necessary component of making the big bucks.

Every so often I'll meet some youngins with enough wits about them to ask me what they should focus on if they want to be rich, or sometimes I'll get these questions from parents who want to guide their children in the right direction to set them up for financial success. My answer is always the same: "Learn how to sell. Learn how to market. Learn how to invest. And learn those things *very well*. Period."

As you dive into the world of sales, marketing, and investing, you'll likely find that you're much better at one than the others. Even though most people view me as a successful investor, my strongest suit is as a marketer and always will be. It's also the avenue that I have the most burning desire for.

For you, though, sales may be your special gift. And within sales, there are a number of subcategories such as face-to-face, webinars, live seminars and events, and managing sales teams. Also, learning the art of copywriting for sales letters, brochures, and websites is probably the most refined and valuable of these skills because you can sell to millions of people at one time without ever personally meeting any them . . . yet can lead to mass sales.

Or, investing may be your thing. There are multiple facets to this area. I look at investing as having two main "umbrellas": real estate, which includes flipping and buy-and-hold passive income strategies; and trading the markets, which includes stocks, bonds, options, futures, and so on. That's about it.

These broad categories are just as vague as if I told you "fruits" and "vegetables." Under fruits, there are bananas, apples, oranges, and a bunch of others—but there are also subcategories. For example, in the apple category, there's Granny Smith, Fuji, Honeycrisp, Gala, Red Delicious, and the list goes on. So when thinking of "real estate" and "trading the markets," think of them like "fruits" and "vegetables" and their subcategories as *niches*. The real money in investing is through these subcategories. That's where you'll make your fortune.

As an example, you won't do that well only being a real estate investor unless you have some kind of specialty. For me, I've done single-family residential (SFR) flipping and later specialized in apartment-building acquisitions for long-term passive income. Lately, I've been working with an even more specialized type of real estate investment with office-building conversions, which is more of a "hybrid" real estate investing and cash-flow business. There are quite a few subcategories for real estate investing and additional sub-subcategories within them. The more you specialize and get really good at your chosen niche, the wealthier you will become.

Before Considering Any Business, Know Thy Numbers!

It makes me shake my head every time I drive past a closed business with a real estate brokerage sign in the window because I know that if the entrepreneur who started the business took the time to do some basic math for five minutes, he or she wouldn't have had to suffer such a dismal business mistake.

For example, just the other day I drove past a business I knew would fail within a short time. It was a shop selling custard dessert cups in a high-end neighborhood in a storefront much too large for its business type. And it made me ask myself this one question: "Why don't some people do their basic numbers before they start their businesses?" Just five minutes with a calculator would tell them if a low-end product offering such as ice cream, custard cups, juice, or milkshakes would make money or not.

My advice for *you* is to start with the monthly rent of the unit you'll have to lease to sell your product out of. Then, ask yourself how many items per day you have to sell just to keep up on your monthly rent, let alone the cost of inventory, utilities, staff, insurance, and the rest of the gamut. You'd have to sell quite a few ice-cream cones, custard cups, bottles of juice, or milkshake creations just to cover the rent, not to mention anything else that is pertinent to running a successful business.

Retail storefront space in my area goes for about five dollars per square foot. That's cheap compared to some areas in California. For a 1,000-square-foot location, that's five grand per month, not including pass-through or common-area maintenance fees. If each order is around five bucks, you'd have to sell over a thousand units per month just to make your rent and additional leasing fees. That doesn't include having employees or keeping your electricity on.

This is why I like to avoid local retail business ideas unless they're highly profitable. These kinds of businesses pigeonhole you into a local area where you're limited to people passing by or those who are within a drivable distance from you. This is not a good marketing plan, especially since the entire world is at our fingertips thanks to the internet. Why go small when you can sell to the entire world? Instead of thinking small, my friend, think big!

Getting Started with OPM

It would be great if we were taught as kids how money works, but unfortunately, we rarely are. The reality is that you need to make the effort to learn about it on your own. If you don't, you'll probably find yourself in financial trouble fairly early on.

I started talking about mortgage amortizations with my daughter when she was in the first grade. I talked to her about how loans and credit cards work. And I told her how to use Other People's Money (OPM) for maximum financial leverage. She usually stared at me with a look of confusion, but I figured it would start to sink in at some point, consciously or subconsciously, and at least she'd know whom she could go to for financial advice when she needed it.

You might have some of the same reactions to a few aspects of the world of high finance—in particular, getting started using OPM. It begins with having really good personal credit. And by really good, I mean getting that mid-FICO score up to 750 or higher. (There are three credit bureaus: Experian, Equifax, and Transunion. Your mid-FICO is the middle score of all three.) That's the baseline for building something we call business or corporate credit. You'll need a strong personal credit base to even start a business credit profile.

Your next step is to form a corporation in your home state. You can Google attorney-managed services such as LegalZoom.com or AmeriLawyer.com, who can help bring your costs down to only a couple hundred dollars in many cases.

When forming your corporation online, you may want to ask for an extra service to help you get an Employer Identification Number (EIN) for your new corporation. This is essentially your corporation's Social Security number. Your EIN is required to help you build your corporate credit, just as your personal Social Security number helps you build your personal credit.

Building corporate credit over the past few decades has changed a lot. I recommend putting your company's EIN on every business credit card and loan. That way, your credit activity will automatically go on your Experian business profile without you paying extra fees and without you doing anything to build and manage a profile.

When you start getting into bigger business loans, a D-U-N-S number will be requested on your loan application. If you go to DandB.com, you'll be able to access a free D-U-N-S number to use for these applications.

This is the ground floor for leveraging OPM to start or expand your positive cash flow.

Who Really Needs a Corporation?

Everyone who's in business needs to have their enterprise incorporated in their home state—absolutely everyone! If you plan on working at home as a freelancer, perhaps as a graphic designer or bookkeeper, you need to form a corporation. If you plan on opening an online store like eBay or Etsy, you need to form a corporation. If you plan on offering a service, even dog-walking or window washing, you need to form a corporation. You need to form one because you'll be doing things to make money. Even if you work for somebody and are happy with your job but you have a side business related to some other avenue of income, you need to form a corporation for it.

As with new babies, you must think of a name for your corporation. My suggestion is something generic and nondescript such as Jemika International Inc. or Barracuda Enterprises Ltd. You can create your own word for the corporate name by combining two different words. Look for a name that doesn't reveal what you sell, do, or promote. That way you have options as to what types of corporate activities you want to engage in if you're not yet quite sure, and also to keep the door open for new opportunities.

Once you decide on your corporate name, you can then narrow down the type of business you want to get into and register something called a "DBA," or "doing business as" with your county. You can add any descriptive business name you wish, and it will be filed under your main corporate umbrella entity. For example, your generic corporate name could be Power House International Inc., which could mean just about anything, and then your narrowed-down DBA name could be Seaside Residential Solar Energy or Tiger Warriors School of Martial Arts, both of which could be reasonable fits under Power House.

Many people ask me why they shouldn't just form a corporation in Nevada, where the annual fees for a corporation are much smaller than, for example, the minimum $800 annual fee in California or wherever they live. The answer is: To be legally compliant, your corporation needs to be in the state in which you're transacting most of your business. If Nevada officials find out that you're incorporated there but running your business out of your apartment in Miami, you could be charged with interstate-commerce violations. So make sure to be legally compliant in everything you do.

A Perfect Blend of Aggressive and Passive Income

There are really only a few things that you'll use to start your new life of financial freedom: business or investing. Ideally, at some point, you'll do both once you gain traction in one or the other.

For example, you could start a home-based e-commerce business that becomes hugely successful and then eventually start channeling some of your profits into buying small apartment buildings that you'll keep for your long-term wealth.

So where do you begin? First, remember not to follow somebody else's path for making money because the likelihood that it'll be a perfect fit for you as well is pretty slim. Being your own boss doesn't just apply when you have your enterprise up and running; it applies right now, at this very moment—along with a trusty sidekick, which would be *me*. If you want to be a self-made, self-reliant, grassroots entrepreneur, I'm the woman who can help you! There are two main strategies for making money:

1. **Aggressive Income Strategies:** These are short-term, where you control how little or how much you make—for example, through an online business, day trading, or flipping real estate. Aggressive income strategies usually point you toward actively selling, marketing, and managing your enterprise on a daily basis, much like that of a regular job.

2. **Passive Income Strategies:** These are long-term, where the market mostly controls how much you make—not you. The only long-term one I recommend in full confidence is investing in real estate with the intent of getting passive income from your tenants—you don't really get to control this income because the market dictates what rents are going for at any given time. "Passive" also suggests that there's little work for you to do, ideally because the perfect property manager is taking care of everything so you don't have to.

Get a "Feel" for Your Niche

"Aggressive" as in aggressive income strategies, means that you get to choose how little or how much you want to make depending on how much time, effort, and energy you're willing to put in. In more than two decades as an entrepreneur, I've found that it comes down to this short list of ideas that fit well with this strategy:

- Sell things through your own website and/or direct-mail marketing, either consumable products like skin-care or health supplements, or recurring-information products such as investment newsletters.

- Sell things through a large third-party online platform like Amazon or Walmart.

- Become a day trader.

- Flip real estate.

- Join a profitable network-marketing organization.

Whichever business idea resonates with you, go about it in a way so that you can *leverage your resources in the best way possible.* This means stretching your abilities, talents, and time to make big dollars without needing an army of staff; otherwise, you'll get yourself into a human-resources and customer-capacity nightmare.

Go through the list above slowly, and trust your gut. Take out a pad of paper and write down how you *feel* about each item. If something feels exciting and exhilarating to you, then it's definitely worth looking into more closely and drilling down to a specific plan. If you feel a knot in your stomach, it's definitely *not* the right opportunity for you despite how much you could potentially make, so don't give it another thought.

Next, we have passive income strategies. Since this type of business activity will come later on, you can hold off on it for now. However, if you'd like to get a head start, tap into your feelings about this short list of moneymaking endeavors that fit in this category, and see if any resonate with you:

- Buy and hold passive income real estate on the residential side, including residential-commercial properties like apartment buildings and mobile-home parks.

- Buy and hold passive income real estate on the commercial side—I call this "commercial-commercial" investing—including office-building space, industrial/warehouse "condos," and retail storefronts, among others.

- Buy and hold long-term stocks, bonds, REITs, and other investment commodities.

For me, there are only a handful of things on these two lists that truly excite me: selling products via my own website, direct-mail marketing, and working with real estate. But just because I have an affinity for certain wealth-building strategies doesn't mean they're right for you. *Trust your gut.*

I have one more unofficial category that I've never publicly revealed before. It's what I call my secret, "hybrid" aggressive-passive strategies:

- Invest in self-storage property. This is a business and real estate holding rolled into one. You need staff to aggressively sell unit space, truck rentals, bubble wrap, tape, boxes, and whatever else, but you will also passively collect monthly rents. This hybrid is quite profitable too.

- Invest in virtual offices. This is also a business and real estate holding bundled together. Lately I've been working with office buildings and converting them into virtual offices for start-ups and small businesses; and specialized, shared professional suites for attorneys, CPAs, psychologists, and the like.

- Invest in a shared space in a beauty salon. This is a business with beauty-service professionals including hairstylists, nail artists, massage therapists, and cosmetologists who run their own "micro" businesses within a "macro" salon or spa. These professionals rent approximately 150 to 400 square feet each at prices ranging from $800 to $1,500 *or more* per month, depending on the appeal of the property.

- Invest in assisted-living facilities for seniors. This property type is in demand today more than ever before because of an increase in our aging population. It requires many layers of legalities that are not for the faint of the heart. However, financially, the payout can be mind-blowing.

- Invest in a sports bar/restaurant. This hybrid can be a really profitable enterprise if done correctly, particularly if you own the building. Yes, it can be expensive to start and operate. And yes, this does require some restaurant- or bar-management experience. But what's also true is that there are huge profit margins: an owner can easily walk away with a minimum of a million bucks a year.

You're just at the starting point, so you don't have to decide anything right now. These are only ideas for you to mull over with confidence that with my more than two decades in the world of business, I know what works to make millionaires . . . as well as what is a complete waste of time.

My wheelhouse has always been marketing information products such as courses and systems to help people better their lives in a significant way while they're investing on the side. Publishing has been the industry that has given me the most success and wealth over the years.

Ideally, you'll zero in (or rather *feel in*) on what excites you the most. Then begin walking your own path, *feeling and knowing* that you'll be guided with a sense of purpose and discipline to gain financial freedom.

The path that moves you may have nothing to do with what I've suggested in this chapter, and that's A-OK. The important part in all this is that you focus on what you're feeling called to do and how you can be of service in a meaningful way. What is your *big idea*? What is your *big dream*? Write it down. You'll know it's the right path if you find yourself absolutely thrilled by the thought of attaining your burning desire. Whatever that is for you, you'll be farther ahead than most everyone else, many of whom are just going through the motions, not knowing what they want in life. Once you identify *exactly* what you want, the next step is to *get* it!

Chapter Six

THE FIFTH STEP TOWARD RICHES: IT'S IN YOUR IMAGINATION

Imagination is everything. It is the preview of life's coming attractions.

—ALBERT EINSTEIN

When you're a businessperson, musician, writer, artist, or anyone else suddenly graced by inspiration, where does it come from? Is there a trick to getting this seemingly unpredictable form of creativity and wisdom to reveal itself more abundantly? Yes, there *is* a trick to it that starts with understanding nature. Here is Napoleon Hill's understanding, as written in *Think and Grow Rich*:

> The imagination is literally the workshop wherein are fashioned all plans created by man. The impulse, the DESIRE, is given shape, form, and ACTION through the aid of the imaginative faculty of the mind. It has been said that men can create anything which he can imagine.
>
> Through the aid of his imaginative faculty, man has discovered, and harnessed, more of Nature's forces during the past fifty years than during the entire history of the human race, previous to that time. He has conquered the air so completely, that the birds are a poor match for him in flying. He has harnessed the ether, and made it serve as a means of

instantaneous communication with any part of the world. He has analyzed, and weighed the sun at a distance of millions of miles, and has determined, through the aid of IMAGINA-TION, the elements of which it consists. He has discovered that his own brain is both a broadcasting, and a receiving station for the <u>vibration</u> of thought, and he is beginning now to learn how to make practical use of this discovery.

◈═══◈

In the earlier story about my burning desire to leave high school early, I was subconsciously calling out for "a" solution. It just so happened that I was walking past those two girls as I was leaving the gym, who just so happened to be talking about "the" solution.

Merely coincidental? *Coincidence* comes from the word *coincide*, which means "to correspond in position, meet, or intersect," so it's kind of odd that we've changed the meaning from "to correspond or intersect" to "a remarkable concurrence of events or circumstances without apparent casual connection."

Guidance and solutions—if you listen closely and open your eyes wide—are given to you in the form of reasoned thoughts, flashes of inspiration, dreams, seeming randomness, and other ways you're not even aware of.

I don't believe in happenstance. Rather, I believe that our lives, as chaotic as they may seem at times, are beautifully orchestrated in some kind of articulately planned performance for all of us to participate in, learn from, and grow with as spiritual beings.

The Akashic Records and How You Can Essentially "Tap into" Your Future

I recently watched an incredible documentary that was mind-blowing and a real eye-opener. It was about *cosmic consciousness* and tapping into the Akashic records. While it's kind of complicated to explain exactly what this means, what I found most incredible was the simple story of a woman named Baba Vanga, the Nostradamus of the Balkans.

Baba Vanga, at the age of twelve, was swept away by a rogue storm that came out of nowhere. The storm violently tossed her small body around; and in the process, layers of sand caked in her eyes, permanently damaging her sight. She was found two days later, lying on the ground, half-dead, but mysteriously, that is also when she received her first vision into the future.

Her presence is still with us. She has made some incredible predictions including the fall of the World Trade Center on 9/11, the fact that our forty-fourth US president would be African American, and that China would become the next superpower. She can see the circumstances under which people are born, what will happen throughout their lives, and how they'll die. It has been said that the reason Baba Vanga and other prophets can predict the future is that the past, present, and future *have already occurred*, and this information is already stored in the Akashic records.

When I've had my own visions, they've really puzzled me—that is, until I discovered the Akashic records. For instance, a few months ago I had an astounding dream about being in an underwater restaurant/hotel. I remember telling a friend how pure and refreshing the oxygen was in this underwater dome, and how the whole experience was the coolest thing ever! Then I began to think about it: with climate change and the destruction of our ozone layer, the likelihood of colonizing a place like Mars seems zilch since we cannot survive its atmosphere. So, since we already have a home here on Earth with the infrastructure and technology needed to survive, I believe it makes perfect sense to use underwater domes to guarantee our survival as a human race in the future.

Then I found out that Baba Vanga had predicted that we'd have underwater civilizations by 2130. It made me smile, and suddenly things began to make more sense to me: dreams, ideas, thoughts, and predictions come from a place that we can all tap into. How else can we explain multiple people getting the same idea at the same time while being a continent or two apart—back before there was the internet, telephones, or any other type of almost-instant communication?

For example, Guglielmo Marconi and Nikola Tesla *both* invented the radio in 1895 at the same time, even though Tesla got the credit as far as patents were concerned. Both Alexander Graham Bell and Antonio Meucci invented the telephone in 1876 at the *same time*, even though Bell got the credit. Einstein's revelation wasn't just *his* work but was also independently revealed by William Sutherland in 1905, both at the *exact same time*, but Einstein got the credit for it. These are just a few of the thousands upon thousands of "coincidences."

It would seem that we have no control over much of anything if everything is already predestined. But does that mean there really is no "free will"? Is everything laid out on a track with little or no leeway to alter its course?

No, I don't believe so. I think of life as a paint-by-numbers kit: There are a bunch of lines, but you get your choice about which colors to paint with, and there's nothing stopping you from coloring outside the lines. Or, you could start over from scratch and create your own unique painting. So yes, you *do* have choices—many, many choices. You can choose to stay on track or you can jump the tracks!

In order to tap into a bigger vision for your life or the world at large, you must get yourself into that place where these thoughts and inspirations exist. You cannot possibly expect to find these magical solutions using the same thinking with the same tired old ideas you've been relying on for too many years.

As Albert Einstein famously said, "We cannot solve our problems with the same thinking we used when we created them." This is particularly true if you feel depressed, "locked in" to a certain destiny, or cornered, without any viable options. It's tricky, though. You can't possibly "think" about freeing solutions while having limiting thoughts that give you a sense of hopelessness, which only serves to attract *more* low-vibrational frequency traps. The only way out of the doldrums is to reach *up* with higher vibrations.

The way I see it, to access the brilliance and genius of Source Energy, you have to aim for creative imagination instead of just regurgitating what's been rattling around in your brain for years. Even though there could be some productive ideas that you've pieced together over time, your best thinking will come from a new and higher place that can only be reached by raising your vibratory levels and getting into the Zone.

Without access to this higher level, your endeavors will be mediocre at best. They'll be centered on what's already in your mind, limited by what you've personally seen, experienced, and remembered. To be extraordinary, you have to access dynamic creative sparks from somewhere well beyond your physical, emotional, and mental limitations.

My Secret for Getting into the Zone

Just about all of us get stuck in a rut at one time or another, feeling like we're swirling in confusion and indecision and that it's impossible to figure out, let alone make, the next moves in our lives.

However, I know a way to get past all this and into the Zone. It begins with understanding that *being stuck is a symptom of being disconnected from Source Energy.* Therefore, to be clear and decisive, and get connected, you will automatically know in which direction to move when you're in that high, vibratory, universal energy flow.

Following is a beautiful exercise to actually shift you into the Zone. It involves meditating for fifteen minutes while doing deep-breathing exercises. I admit that I've had a difficult time meditating in the way it was originally devised—that is, clearing my mind and just "being." I've never been able to do that, since I have a very active imagination. It's as if my thought "freight train" just never stops barreling through my mind. Believe me, I've tried many times and have always ended up feeling that meditation isn't for me.

Then I discovered deep breathing along with meditation, and everything changed. I found it easy to simply close my eyes and focus on my breathing. Yes, thoughts breeze in as usual, but with the focus on my breathing, I find it pretty simple to send those thoughts right back out where they came from, usually by way of a long exhalation.

I start out with a very simple breathing technique called the *earth breath*. This is when you breathe in and out through your nose very slowly, deeply, and consciously. You can also do the *air breath*, where you breathe in and out through your mouth. By focusing on either of these breaths with your eyes closed, you'll begin to feel your mind and body lighten up. After fifteen full minutes, if done consciously, you'll feel the natural high from being in the Zone.

Another approach I use is the Emotional Freedom Technique (EFT). Years ago I went to an event where a man by the name of Nick Ortner, author of the book *The Tapping Solution*, was speaking. During his presentation, he had everyone participate in a crash course on how tapping works. It was the first time I'd ever heard of such a thing and initially thought it was weird to be doing this "tapping" thing in a room with hundreds of people. But when I was done with the short exercise, I felt out-of-this-world wonderful. I had never felt so exhilarated in such a short amount of time in my entire life! And the effects of this one-time tapping exercise kept me uplifted for about two days.

Ever since then, I've been tapping as an additional method to help me get into the Zone, especially when I'm feeling blue or anxious. Tapping can also be used to help alleviate deep emotional, and even physical, pain.

Once you're in the Zone, creative ideas can surge into your head, or they may arise later when you least expect them. And sometimes they aren't ready to appear for a long time—these golden nuggets like to come to you when you've let go, stopped trying so hard, and have immersed yourself in feeling phenomenal.

Here's another approach that works well. Before getting into the Zone, write down a short list of things that you're interested in pursuing. Maybe you're not sure in which direction to go as far as potential business ventures are concerned, or you have a few possibilities under consideration but just don't know which one to choose. When your list is ready, bring yourself into the Zone; this higher vibrational level will immediately tell you which of those options is best for you—if any. Maybe you'll end up with a completely new and amazing idea instead!

When you're in the Zone, you can also look at all the areas of your life, one by one, and get a vibrational feel for each one. When you really focus on each area, you'll immediately know how to enhance them. If any idea gives you a sinking feeling in your stomach, then it's not a direction to go in, despite how great it looks on paper.

However, if you feel exhilarated, like you're flying high when thinking about a certain idea, then it's one you need to go for even if you have doubts. Here's the way Napoleon Hill explained it in *Think and Grow Rich*:

> This earth, every one of the billions of individual cells of your body, and every atom of matter, *began as an intangible form of energy.*
>
> Through the combination of energy and matter, has been created everything perceptible to man, from the largest start which floats in the heavens, down to, and including man, himself.
>
> Strange and paradoxical as it may seem, the "secret" is NOT A SECRET. Nature, herself, advertises it in the earth on which we live, the stars, and the planets suspended within our view, in the elements above and around us, in every blade of grass, and every form of life within our vision.
>
> Nature advertises this "secret" in the terms of biology, in the conversion of a tiny cell, so small that it may be lost on the point of a pin, into the HUMAN BEING now reading this line. The conversion of desire into its physical equivalent is, certainly, no more miraculous!

❖▭▭▭❖

When you're in the Zone, no matter how much your lower-vibratory being has tried to convince you what is or isn't possible in your life, *all things become possible instantly.* The Universe will begin to conspire on your behalf to make these happen through the "microscopic bits of matter" that will be "organized and arranged in an orderly fashion" to make your dreams come true. Any negativity allowed in will disrupt the art of this unification by interfering with the microscopic bits already lining up to manifest your grandest desires.

Stanford University has done related experiments proving that directed thoughts produce physical energy measured in frequencies (two to thirty hertz). This energy can be transmitted nearby or thousands of miles away, through unobstructed air or steel walls. It can also affect the molecular structure of matter. It has been scientifically proven that thoughts are both electrostatic and magnetic energy, which explains why being at higher vibrational levels can literally *magnetize* other higher vibrational things, people, and circumstances to you.

Getting in and being in the Zone is the peak time to visualize and *feel* your burning desire coming to fruition, with a *knowing* that it will manifest. You may think that you're just sitting there dreaming about your goals, but your thoughts have a hard-core punch that you might not have ever considered. This is why you can actually shorten your life if you constantly think about negative things, have lingering doubts about yourself, and stay trapped in despondency over the way your life has turned out. This power can only bring in more of what you're thinking and feeling, which means that the only cure for a life that sucks is to channel that power to pull in a fantastic life instead.

It is a fairly simple equation: You have an idea and you put it "out there." Then you listen for and feel ideas, thoughts of inspiration, and sparks of creativity to get your ideas to materialize. When they arrive, you must move on them quickly so that they form a vacuum that will pull in *more* inspiration and keep you moving forward toward their manifestation.

Taking This to the Next Level

If you want to make a million dollars, that money already exists somewhere. It's just a matter of moving it into your bank account. Since money is a form of energy, simply raise your vibration and fine-tune your visualization for it to flow right in. There's a link here; the key is to visualize whatever you need in order to keep your high vibrational energy connection in place. If visualizing a river of millions of dollars flooding your bank account is how you get there, so be it.

This likely won't be a literal portrayal of how the money will actually end up in your bank account, but your visualization doesn't have to be literal, but rather, via wire transfers, checks, PayPal, and so on, but it *does* need to reflect your best representation of what you want to see happen while allowing yourself to remain open to Source Energy. I've found that being more vague and more metaphoric is a better way for me to visualize than trying to be very specific.

I've also found that literal visualization can backfire. For example, if you're visualizing the actual transfer of a million bucks to you from others, you may be inclined to see thoughts of them giving you a check and then you driving to the bank to make a deposit. The problem with this visualization is that you may begin to feel resistance to any details that seem out of place. Your conscious mind might say, "Nobody writes a personal check for a million dollars. It will be a bank wire. No, it will be a cashier's check." You begin throwing up walls, disconnecting from Source Energy, and getting out of alignment as far as attracting the money you want.

A better way is to just imagine something like a river or rain pouring into your account and you checking your balance to find that it shows a million-dollar deposit. Then, home in at that moment on how you will *feel* when this situation occurs. Hold on to that feeling, because *that* is where the power is, not in the mechanics.

Feel a ball of warm light expanding between your heart and gut. Then feel it expanding beyond your body and into the Universe. *Know* that what you want has already happened. At the end of each visualization session, say, "I let go and let God, with the trust that what I want manifests for me in the highest and best way and for the good of all concerned." And that's the end of it. Do this every evening until you get what you want.

Quite honestly, children can be much more powerful and speedy creators than adults because they have fewer emotional barriers, preconceived notions, and judgments that can considerably slow down the process. In fact, in many cases, adults' resistance can bring manifestations to a complete stop. Even worse, many of us simply aren't clear about what we want. When I was a kid and wanted to move to California, I was very clear about it. Very concise. Very specific. Very focused. I don't think I've ever been that clear about anything I've wanted since then.

As an adult, you might fancy yourself as having more "sophisticated" desires. Maybe you do, but the problem is that this sophistication often adds layers of complications that *simple, pinpointed clarity* is free of. The lesson is: *Be crystal clear about what you want, and focus on manifesting one thing at a time.* Scattered visualizations and desires will likely get you nowhere.

If you find when you close your eyes that you just can't visualize images, draw on a piece of paper what you imagine your dream to look like. Focus on the *feeling state* of what it's like to already have what you want, while at the same time keeping your high vibratory connection aligned with Source Energy.

At the end of your visualization session, *let it go.* Just know that it will be taken care of when the time comes. Let go and let God. Don't give your visualization another thought until the following evening when you do your next visualization session.

Pay attention to any negative thoughts you might toss around, such as, *Who am I to think I can have something like this anyway?* Or, *I can't suffer through another day at this job.* Or, *Where is the successful business I've always wanted?*

Each time you immerse yourself in this low vibratory energy, you essentially negate all the high vibratory energy you put into your creative visualization the night before. If the negativity finds its way in, plan on starting over until you can flush out all those damaging thoughts. When you sense them starting to intrude, say to yourself: *I know they're coming, so I am just going to relax!* Then let go of them immediately before the lowly energy can sink its teeth into the positive traction you've already banked.

The 10 Steps of Powerful Creative Visualization

Here are the precise steps you need to take to get *anything you want* through creative visualization:

Step 1: At night when you're ready to go to sleep, disconnect from all electronics, turn all the lights off, quiet any noise, and comfortably lie in bed on your back. Ideally you're ready to slip into slumber, but you're not so tired that you can't complete a ten- to fifteen-minute creative visualization session.

Step 2: Close your eyes and begin breathing deeply, in and out through your nose. This is the *earth* breath and is perfect for grounding. If you find that breathing through your mouth is better for you, then switch to that—this is the *air* breath and is perfect for visualization and manifestation. Push all thoughts out of your head while feeling your muscles relax, one part of your body at a time. I like to start at my feet and move my way up my legs, pelvis, torso, and shoulders to the top of my head. There's no right or wrong way to do this. Just be aware of relaxing your entire body and making sure you have no tension.

Step 3: Begin thinking about what you want to attract. Feel your heart and abdomen areas expand with a feeling of joy and excitement about the burning desire you wish to manifest. Feel your energy vibrating at a higher level as you immerse yourself in the exhilaration of your desire, allowing the Universe to work out the hows and whys. This step is only about using the excitement and thrill of your desire as a "prop" to lift your vibration to a higher level.

Step 4: Begin to visualize how it will be to have successfully manifested your burning desire. What does the end result look like? How does it feel? What are you doing in this "snapshot"? Really tap into the *feeling state* of this experience, as it needs to be one of pure joy, excitement, exhilaration, and fun!

Step 5: Visualize your heart and abdomen areas filling up with a ball of light that is getting warmer and larger as it mirrors your joy, happiness, and excitement. Feel this light get larger and larger until it expands outside of your body.

Step 6: If you like, you can send this ball of light out into the Universe through the power of your mind, and then think to yourself or say out loud: "I let go and let God fulfill this desire, and trust that it is happening with the highest and best good for all involved." Feel the sense of letting it go into higher hands.

Step 7: Take some final breaths, and express gratitude for how awesome the Universe is. Then let it all go.

Step 8: Keep your mind off of your burning desire until the next evening. You'll keep doing this creative visualization night after night until your desire manifests itself. If you're persistent, it will come to fruition before you know it.

Step 9: Look for thoughts of inspiration and signs of guidance coming to you, and feel their power when you recognize them.

Step 10: If you're inspired to call someone, post something, go somewhere, pick up a magazine, visit someone's house, or whatever the intuitive feeling may be, *do it*. Follow through with your instincts, and take action!

And that, my friend, is how easy it is to get what you want.

Feeling *Is the Secret*

Neville Goddard, a forward thinker in the New Age movement, wrote a very short book called *Feeling Is the Secret*. The title basically describes what the book is about. You absolutely must get into the high-vibe *feeling state* of having what you want, to the point where you feel as if you're *becoming* what it is you want before you even have it, and then ultimately feel that *you are* what you want. In your mind, body, and spirit, there is no separation of time and space; you become *one* with your burning desire.

Now, I'm not going to lie to you: if you're sweeping floors as a minimum-wage employee at a fast-food restaurant, it's going to be difficult trying to think beyond that, unless you begin using your bridge affirmations before affirming that you're a successful business owner or whatever your goal is.

There's another secret to dealing with the major disparity between the reality of how your life is right now and the positive affirmations related to how you *want* your life to be, going forward. It took me years to find the answer to this enigma, but here it is: *Raise your energy, with a great sense of excitement about your burning desire.*

Let's use the example of you wanting to create a successful business of your own. Think about the excitement of owning and running this new business. Think about how incredible your life is when you can work your own hours, afford all the toys you want, and call the shots. Focus on the *excitement only*. Allow this feeling to *raise your energy*. It's best not to have any specific pictures in your head about what your new business looks like. Don't think about the "how" or the "when." Leave that to the Universe to work out and to guide you. Instead, focus on raising your vibes with pure excitement. And that's it. Let it go, *and let it happen!*

Whenever I have difficulty raising my vibrations to a higher level with my usual fifteen-minute meditation and deep-breathing practice, I switch gears and think of something that's coming up on my calendar that I'm really excited about. For instance, if there's an event I'm scheduled to attend, I think of all the people I'll meet, the new things I'll learn, and the industry heavy-hitters I'll network with. By focusing on the event, my energy levels go through the roof almost instantly.

I then shift my excitement about the event over to my burning desire. Parlaying this high vibrational energy keeps me in the Zone, which allows me to manifest my burning desire with this same high-flying vibratory state. I no longer experience self-doubt, self-criticism, self-deprecation, or anything else I may throw at myself with negative self-talk . . . because these types of emotions, feelings, and thoughts cannot coexist with an ultra-high vibratory energy level. The secret, then, is to get yourself into that high vibrational feeling state *before* thinking about what you want to create. By doing so, it's literally impossible for low vibratory feelings and thoughts to interfere with your goal of making your burning desire a reality.

Imagine how incredibly powerful it would be to remain in this high vibratory state as much as possible, even if you aren't focusing on a specific desire that you wish to manifest. This state of being allows you to access infinite guidance from the Universe. It allows for thoughts of inspiration to flow down to you with ease and speed.

Become So Powerful That You Can Manifest with Your Mind

Let's simplify this a little and talk about actually *thinking* something into reality, almost instantaneously. This is possible once you're able to tap into your power at will, which, by the time you finish reading this book, you will have the tools to do.

Recently I manifested three simple things into my life with just my thoughts. The first was a lamp for my office. The fluorescent lights had gone out a couple of weeks before, and I was using a small battery-operated lamp next to my desktop computer. The fluorescent lights cast so much glare that I was relieved when they went out, but I didn't know what kind to replace them with. I thought in general terms, *Wouldn't it be great to create a softer ambience when I'm working?* Then I immediately let go of that thought with the idea that I'd go online or pick up a lamp at a store when I had the chance. A week later, a lamp in a box was delivered to my doorstep. It was the perfect gift from a business colleague!

The next thing I manifested was an oversize mug. I'd started drinking a lot of hot tea and found that I wanted a bigger cup to hold more liquid. I thought to myself, *Wouldn't it be great to have a really big mug for my tea?* I thought about how I'd buy one of those oversize mugs the next time I went shopping. Less than a week later, someone gave me a beautiful white-and-gold celestial-patterned oversize mug.

And finally, I was thinking about how I'd like to eat Alpha Bits cereal. I hadn't had it in a long time and was craving this child-hood favorite for some reason. I thought to myself, *Next time I'm online, I'll order the cereal since the grocery stores around here don't carry it.* Then I let the thought go. A few days later, two boxes of Alpha Bits were delivered to my door. I hadn't ordered them! A friend had sent them to me as a joke, thinking he was being com-ical, and it turned out that it was exactly what I wanted.

In my world, there's nothing unusual about this kind of man-ifestation. I notice that the more I put myself into this higher vibrational state of being, my thoughts automatically begin man-ifesting in these kinds of ways. However, when I'm going through bouts of feeling low and depressed, I cut myself off from this mag-ical flow—from enjoying business profits to meeting happy people to finding a parking space at the mall. That is, many of the things I want and need are *cut off* when I allow my vibrational energies to dip into lower levels. I'm 100 percent certain that it's the same for you. If you aren't getting what you want—from the simplest to the most complex things—it's because you're vibrating way too low to (a) tap into the flow of those good things coming into your life, and (b) receive brilliant ideas and inspirational thoughts about the next steps to follow through on to manifest more of what you want.

When you keep your energy levels raised as high as possible, you'll find manifestation and creation happening *all the time* in alignment with Source Energy. You have access to it right now, at this very moment, as you read this sentence. You just have to lift any low energy into high energy; it is *always* there and never goes away.

What typically happens over time is that life can grind us down. It can make us cynical, jaded, angry, anxiety ridden, and depressed because of the many challenges that have personally affected us over the years, not to mention the many issues in the world that have indirectly affected us. It's enough to make the most sane person a little loopy now and again. This negative perception of reality is what unplugs us from Source Energy. *But all we have to do is plug ourselves back in.*

It's one thing to manifest one simple object such as a coffee mug. It's more complicated with a complex creation that often takes time, effort, and energy over the years to build in a way that matches the end result of your burning desire.

Understand that we're on a slow-moving Earth plane of existence. It takes a little time to get the momentum rolling to move mountains for your big ideas and dreams. And to do so, you can tap into Source Energy to (1) give you the multimillion-dollar business idea, (2) give you thoughts and inspiration about the first steps to begin building this new business, and (3) give you a push to take action.

If you choose to do nothing at all with the ideas, thoughts, and inspiration given to you from this higher place, they'll dry up, and more important, clog up your pipeline so they stop coming to you altogether. Source Energy, after all, will find no purpose in sending you all those good ideas when they could be going to others who've proven themselves to be movers and shakers.

Getting What You Want Through Your Book of Magic

The night I graduated with my MFA, my then–significant other gave me a mystical-looking leather journal with blank pages inside. It seemed like a prop right out of a Harry Potter flick. I flung the journal on a bookshelf where it stayed for two years before I decided to pick it up, dust it off, and make it my *Book of Magic*, as if I really were Dumbledore.

I began by doing daily morning meditations and deep breathing to get myself into the Zone. With my *Book of Magic* by my side, I wrote down all the goals and dreams I wanted to manifest in my life. I drew magic wands and wrote short, enchanting sentences followed by words such as *Wizham!* and other lingo that I made up. I believed that everything I wrote in my *Book of Magic* had already come true. I had *no doubt*.

Within a short time, I started to notice that the things I was writing in my *Book of Magic* were starting to come true! Just for the heck of it, I wrote that I'd manifest $100,000 in thirty days. The money came in ten days later! I wrote that I'd start a brand-new product line that would triple my income. It happened in less than two months. After all these successes, I was acutely aware that if I was 100 percent intent on what I wanted, I would get everything I wrote about in my *Book of Magic*.

So then I started cutting out pictures and making a hybrid *Book of Magic* and a dream board all in one. Today, I have to tell you, this process has been nothing short of life changing. It forced me to get crystal clear about what I want. And it's a lot of fun to draw silly wizard pictures and write out enchanting, poetic, "fun-loving spells" in my book.

Maybe it's time you create your own *Book of Magic*. Not only will you become crystal clear about what you want, but you'll be able to further develop those golden nuggets of inspiration. I recommend starting with a journal that looks "magical" on the outside and has blank pages on the inside. Treat it as a "conscious book," knowing that everything you write, paste, or draw in it can come true.

Shazzam!

Chapter Seven

THE SIXTH STEP TOWARD RICHES: CREATING YOUR GRAND PLAN

Success doesn't just happen. It's planned for.

—ANONYMOUS

"A journey of a thousand miles begins with a single step," as the common translation of the well-known Chinese proverb goes. But the literal translation is: "A journey of a thousand miles starts beneath one's feet."

Your journey to where you want to be starts with *where you are right now*. You have everything you need to take your first step, which involves raising your vibration, as we've discussed, while keeping yourself open for the next step to be revealed. Once each step is given to you, it's critical that you act upon it swiftly and with great enthusiasm.

Sometimes you may need to concoct a plan that you *believe* would be the best way to reach your goals, then work your way backward from attainment of your end vision to where you are now. This approach can help launch your journey while you remain flexible and open to potentially better paths and ideas given to you along the way. Trust me when I say that new ideas and inspiration will be given to you once you *take action* and *begin to walk the path*. Sometimes, though, you have to do research and then make the best-educated guess as to the best action. As Napoleon Hill wrote in *Think and Grow Rich*, keep moving forward no matter what:

> If the first plan which you adopt does not work successfully, replace it with a new plan, if this new plan fails to work, replace it, in turn with still another, and so on, until you find a plan which DOES WORK. Right here is the point at which the majority of men meet with failure, because of their lack of PERSISTENCE in creating new plans to take the place of those which fail. The most intelligent man living cannot succeed in accumulating money—nor in any other undertaking—without plans which are practical and workable. Just keep this fact in mind, and remember when your plans fail, that temporary defeat is not permanent failure. It may only mean that your plans have not been sound. Build other plans. Start all over again.

◈═══◈═══◈

Napoleon Hill's idea of "organized planning," as he presented in his book, is limiting in that he talks at great length about finding a job at a company. I believe this was intended to help 1937 post-Depression readers who had survival on their minds. You, though, have more to think about. Working for a company, climbing up the ladder, getting a pension, and living happily ever after in retirement is now largely a fantasy. The most recent near-collapse of our economy in 2008 played a large part in this transformation.

To be successful in today's economy, you need a relatively self-reliant entrepreneurial-based plan, even as an employee. You may want to be a scientist in a research lab, a teacher at a school, an attorney for the government, a social worker for a nonprofit, a police officer, or a firefighter, but whatever the case, I still suggest that you think of some side business to fall back on to add to your financial freedom. This side business can be anything, including investing in real estate, freelancing, or consulting.

As you may have figured out by now, I'm a huge supporter of entrepreneurship, so I won't be coaxing you along the road of being someone else's employee. That's just not my area of expertise or interest. Since you're reading this book, it probably isn't yours, either.

Having been a wealth trainer since 2001, I've seen thousands of people with a pretext, not a burning desire, to become wealthy. Yet, very few have actually decided that this is really what they want, and even fewer are willing to perform the needed steps to become wealthy. This leaves many individuals sitting on the fence year after year, deciding nothing and doing nothing to increase their fortunes. They usually blame someone else or some other circumstance for why they haven't gotten rich instead of looking in the mirror to see that they're the creators and masters of their own destinies. That would mean taking responsibility for their own lives, and, well, many people don't want to deal with any of *that* nonsense.

The magic of manifesting something starts with *deciding* to do something. Not making a decision with respect to your burning desire equals not manifesting it. If you don't already have some kind of burning desire that you know you want to pursue, it's time to find one.

In prior chapters, we've discussed techniques on how to raise your energy vibration so new ideas and increased abundance will begin flowing into your life—for example, steps to becoming a millionaire. If you haven't gotten that million-dollar idea yet, keep *raising your energy*—which you'll want to do each day anyway—by starting with a quick fifteen-minute morning meditation where you do some deep breathing. At the same time, ask Infinite Intelligence for the perfect inspiration that fits your needs, personality, and preferences. Then let it go. When you least expect it, you just might overhear a couple of little old ladies having a conversation at your local café who will reveal your perfect business idea. *So pay close attention to the signs around you at all times!*

Your inspiration should *burn in your heart and soul*. Once you have this idea, *decide* that you will go through hell or high water for it. *Decide* comes from the Latin word *decidere,* which literally means "to cut off." You cut off other options by virtue of deciding on this one thing only. There is great power in the act of making a firm decision. It is magical, as if you're parting the seas to allow for its safe passage.

Heeding "the Call"

Recently I met with a friend named Mia whom I've known for many years. She'd been a store manager with a well-known chain for more than a decade. The position allowed her almost no free time; and she worked a rigid, near-impossible schedule. She told me that she'd made the decision to leave the company and her solid six-figure annual income, and that she'd never felt more elated in her entire life. Just the act of *deciding* gave her a sense of instant happiness, because it meant "cutting off" her current state of affairs, which made her feel as if she were in prison. The sense of freedom and joy on her face was uplifting. Glowing in this state of bliss, she told me, "I've always done well for myself, and I just *know* I'm destined for much more. So I'm not worried. I know I'll find something else to do that will be much better for me."

I asked her some questions, trying to pinpoint two things: (1) When and why did she decide to give up her secure, high-paying position when the alternative was literally unknown territory? and (2) How did she know there was something more out there for her? Neither question had a defined answer. Her answer was: (1) when she could think about little else; and (2) when her desire for change was so intense that she felt it was her destiny.

You have these experiences too, though you may not be paying attention to them. Like my friend, the call will grow louder and louder until you feel compelled to do something about it. Or, if you do *not* take action, it's likely that some cataclysmic event will occur to force this change upon you, such as the loss of your job, an illness, a relationship breakup, or something else. Clearly it's better to take action on your own when you feel a tug at your gut rather than waiting for the change to be forced upon you.

But you may say, "Well, I don't have the luxury of quitting a job I hate to follow my passion. I have a family to feed, bills to pay—every day and every month."

I understand. Nobody says the steps you take have to be drastic. My friend Mia had been subconsciously preparing for this change in her life for years by saving money so she'd have a financial cushion. Some may argue that she'd already planned for it, even if it wasn't on a fully conscious level: something inside of her began whispering that there was a lot more out there long before she made a conscious decision to move on. After all, she did tell me she always knew she was destined for much more because she'd always felt that to be true in the deepest part of her being. The calling never went away; it just got louder as the years passed, until she couldn't hear herself think about anything else.

For you, making the decision that you want to leave your job or profession and do something more meaningful will be your first order of business. That is your first step: *decide*. Make a decision. This doesn't mean you need to go tell your boss today that you're quitting. It simply means to internally decide that you'll be moving on to do something else, even if you don't know what that something else is. This is where your *shift* begins. You'll be surprised by how many ideas, thoughts of inspiration, and plans are "beamed down" to you once you decide to do something bigger. Decide to become something better. Just decide *something*. That's all you need to do right now. The rest will fall into place in the days and weeks to come.

Organized Planning with a Simple Brainstorming Chart

Once you start to access ideas and thoughts of inspiration from a higher place, write them down. This means you should always have a small pad of paper and a pen handy, especially during the night when things pop into your head or weave themselves into your dreams, because you never know when or where these nuggets will flood into your mind. If you prefer, instead of writing, you can record them on your smartphone or other device. Sometimes these messages are delivered to you through a conversation, or even while you're standing in line at the grocery store and you see a headline on a magazine cover. Or, maybe you bump into an old friend you haven't talked to in years who reminds you of a passion you let slip away.

Once that awesome idea drops in, *do something about it!* Take some kind of immediate action related to it. Don't sit and think about it for six months. Do something about it *now*, even if you're only working with a partial idea so far. The rest will fill in once you start taking action—trust within your soul that you will always be guided in this way.

If you're given a powerful idea and you don't move on it fast (or at all), that same idea will be gifted into somebody else's mind, and that person may run with it, leaving you in the dust. How many times have you said about an invention or an idea: "I thought of that years ago!" Or "That was *my* idea!"

Imagine this scenario: An amazing wiz-bang idea drops into your head, you're off-the-wall ecstatic about it, and you *know* it's the winner you've been looking for. But you feel paralyzed: *OMG, what do I do now?*

Take a large piece of paper and start brainstorming. Draw a small circle in the middle of the page, and inside it, write down the central idea. Say, for example, your multimillion-dollar idea is to start a new clothing line with a unique angle to it. You love the Caribbean islands, the people, the colors, and the clothes, so your unique selling proposition (USP) is to import clothing and handbags from Jamaica and sell them in the United States and internationally. Refining your idea even further, you decide you want to donate a portion of your profits to a special charity in Jamaica to help buy schoolchildren some needed books, supplies, and computers. So you'd write inside the circle: JAMAICAN CLOTHING/ BAGS IMPORTING BUSINESS.

As you begin committing to a central theme, you'll find that more ideas will start to pop into your mind. From the circle, draw a line off to the right. That can be for your first brainstorming branch. Let's say you decide to EDUCATE YOURSELF. Circle those words and have some branches come off that bubble with ideas on how to get educated about your new clothing enterprise. You may decide to take a business trip to Jamaica for a week to immerse yourself in the culture, connect with mom-and-pop clothing manufacturers who can sell you their products wholesale, and get some additional information. So in this first branch under the EDUCATE YOURSELF bubble, you can write something like TRIP TO JAMAICA. Then circle it.

You may have another idea to check into MasterClass.com (which I highly recommend) to watch courses given by clothing-related designers and businesses such as Marc Jacobs and Diane von Furstenberg for ideas on running a successful clothing line. Under EDUCATE YOURSELF, draw another branch and write MASTER CLASS. Then circle it.

Suddenly you may have another idea that you want to draw off to the left. You have a flash of inspiration and call it E-COMMERCE. Underneath that you draw more lines branching out: AMAZON. ETSY. EBAY. MY OWN WEBSITE. Circle each one individually.

From your main circle and straight down the middle, draw another branch. Maybe what comes to mind is: BIZ STRUCTURE. Then circle it. Off that new bubble, you draw another branch: INCORPORATE. Another one: BIZ NAME, and another: DOMAIN FOR BIZ. Then, maybe: HOME OFFICE, BUSINESS CHECKING ACCOUNT, and BUSINESS CARDS.

You'll need a branch named PRODUCTS. Circle it. From there, draw lines for additional branches such as: RESEARCH SUPPLIERS/ MANUFACTURERS IN JAMAICA, FIND PRODUCTS ON JAMAICA TRIP, TAKE PICTURES OF PRODUCTS FOR E-COMMERCE.

This is how your chart might look:

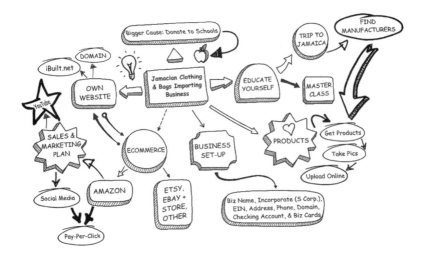

There are a variety of ways to create a brainstorming chart. You might like squares instead of circles, arrows instead of straight lines, or squiggles and highlights. There's no right or wrong way as long as it gives you fodder for your creativity to flow through.

Just get the initial ideas down as fast as they come, free-flowing whatever comes along, and censoring nothing. As you brainstorm, you'll find yourself coming up with the most brilliant and amazing ideas seemingly out of nowhere. This is the truest connection to Source Energy because it means that you're *connected* to it directly, with no blocks, interruptions, or resistance. Stay plugged in as long as you can. Harvest as many golden nuggets of ideas and inspiration while that valve is open.

Breaking Down Your Brainstorming Chart into Usable Baby Steps

I love the idea of baby steps. Don't those words make the most enormous and intimidating task seem doable and even fun? Truth is, most everything can be completed without pressure or stress when broken down to bite-size pieces that can be consistently checked off of your list.

Going back to your brainstorming chart, the overall "theme" of your big idea might seem enormous and intimidating when looked at as a whole. Each of the branches could then be considered smaller bites, and each sub-branch under those, even smaller bites. You can branch out farther to make the bites easier on you. These micro steps may not have all surfaced in your brainstorming, so just add them as you begin organizing your chart into a real action plan.

If you keep your larger tasks without creating manageable micro steps, you're setting yourself up for failure because (1) the big idea as a whole is often overwhelming; and (2) *organizing*, by definition, means assembling various parts into a whole. Therefore, coming up with manageable micro steps isn't just a catchy self-help tip, it's a requirement so that you can make progress.

Say, for example, that you want to write the next Great American Novel. You're inspired. You have a fantastic idea for the storyline. Your characters are lining up in your head. You jot down plot points. You outline your overall structure. And then something happens. You stop. In your excitement, you start fantasizing about it being the next *War and Peace*. Then you psych yourself out: "I can't crank out an epic masterpiece! The odds of a first-time novelist getting published are really small." And then, "I really don't have the time for this. When the kids are grown and out of the house, then I'll write it." You throw the project on the back burner, where it will stay.

Looking at the big picture is perfect when you're doing creative visualization, but when it comes down to getting the job done, you must think in terms of "chunked-down" blocks. For example, if you take only fifteen minutes a day to write your novel, you'll have about one page a day. After a year, that's 365 pages. That's a novel! So, after twelve months, you'll have a first draft.

When you're in that fifteen-minutes-a-day groove writing your novel, one of two things will happen: (1) you'll expand your writing to longer periods, maybe twenty or thirty minutes a day (or even an hour); or (2) you'll at least learn how to write faster to squeeze more into your quarter hour of writing. Either way, you'll likely have your first draft completed in six months to a year, with the goal of presenting it to an agent or publisher.

The way to chunk down your big tasks into fifteen minutes a day begins with outlining a plan. This is when you can minimize each step and substep into those bite-size pieces. The more preparation you do, the easier this process will be. For your novel, do as much outlining as possible before writing. For your business, learn from other experts before executing your business plan. For a new healthful eating regimen, throw away all the junk food in your house, and replace it with healthier choices. Prepare first; then execute.

A word of caution, though: Don't get stuck in preparation purgatory. Some people think they're furthering their project when really they're trapped in an endless loop of verifying, confirming, digging, then revising and doing it all over again. Learn as much as you can, and outline as much as you can. If you've been at it for longer than two or three months, you're likely stuck in a preparation vortex. You need to start doing those fifteen minutes a day, even if you don't have all the pieces in place.

When you commit to doing those fifteen minutes, you'll be surprised by how quickly you can whip together your business empire, Great American Novel, or whatever it is you have a burning desire for.

Chapter Eight

THE SEVENTH STEP TOWARD RICHES: THE POWER OF DECISION

....

Action is the foundational key to all success.

—PABLO PICASSO

....

For years I found myself on a dieting yo-yo. I even made the mistake of taking doctor-prescribed Phentermine, which completely threw off my metabolism, not to mention wreaked havoc with my mood swings. I was desperate to lose weight, especially after having turned forty and seeing the pounds pack on, even though I was hardly eating anything.

Then I began sending out a vibration to the Universe to find the healthiest diet and exercise plan that I'd stick to, and which would make me feel amazing. I no longer cared about squeezing into a bikini; I cared about feeling better, thinking with more clarity, and having more energy.

Shortly thereafter, my daughter chimed in, "Mom, we need to start eating better." *Okay,* I thought, *that's an interesting "signal" from the Universe: maybe it's time to start instituting dietary changes for both of us.* But I was still stuck. No matter how many books I read about healthy eating, I found that the more information I collected, the more confused I became.

Out of nowhere I got a completely unrelated burst of inspiration to cover a tattoo on my lower back with something more goddess-like. During my last marriage, I'd gotten a Detroit "D" tattoo since my husband was from the Motor City, But I came to realize that covering it up would provide a final bit of closure.

I went to see Ray, a wonderfully talented tattoo artist who'd inked my other tats in my mid-thirties. When I walked into his establishment, I was shocked by how much weight he'd lost since I'd last seen him. During the painful two-hour-long tattoo cover-up and replacement, Roy told me all about the changes he'd made in his diet to end up trimmer now than he'd ever been.

"Monica, I'm telling you, losing weight is not that hard. You just have to change the way you think about it. Like, when you go into the grocery store, head straight to the back. You only want the fruits, veggies, and meats—all the stuff on the perimeter. Skip all the processed stuff in the front and middle, with a few exceptions like tuna and beans. Just stay away from the processed stuff."

Ray went on to explain exactly what he was eating and how he was preparing it. However, he did mention that although he'd given up fast food and junk food, he did allow himself to "cheat" a little if he had to.

"That's basically how it works," he told me.

That's it? I thought to myself. Who knew that my tattoo artist would guide me to change my eating habits so that I would not only lose weight but feel more healthy, energetic, and wonderful? Oh, and by the way, I love my new tattoo!

When I got home, I decided to follow Ray's advice. I went through my refrigerator, freezer, and pantry; loaded up large garbage bags with junk food; and carried them out to the trash can. While only a week before I probably would have cringed at the thought of tossing out hundreds of dollars' worth of food, my mind was now ready for a change, and I didn't give my decision a second thought, knowing that improving my life was a million times more valuable than a few bags of food. Within days, my craving for all that junk food disappeared. Once my mind was ready, my body followed. Something *shifted* within me, and I felt as if I were a different person because of it. My focus, energy, and personal power also shifted. These days, I have more stamina and concentration than ever before, which is one reason why my business is booming.

These results prompted me to do further research on health. Some of the information I uncovered is rather startling—for example, how artificial sweeteners, GMOs, processed food, drugs, alcohol, and over-the-counter painkillers dramatically lower our vibrational frequency, obstructing us from manifesting our desires.

When we decide to eat clean, something will "switch" in our brains. It's as if we cross a bridge and don't want to go back in the other direction. When we make the concrete decision to improve our lives, we become different people, in a sense.

This is similar to being in a bad relationship where you're trying to make it work, you're suffering through it, and years go by, but it's not getting better. In fact, it's getting worse. Then one day you take a step back and think to yourself, *I'm going to end this and move on.* Once you decide to take action, you become that different person. You move from being a victim of a situation to being in charge of it. You move from one perspective to a completely different one—*instantly!* In your mind, you've already moved on, even if your former life lingers. Once your mind decides, the Universe will follow.

Making a decision means exercising great power. Even before you take action, you can feel your strength increase just from the act of deciding. When you decide on something important and know it's the right decision, you'll also feel an uplifted vibration; you'll feel out-of-this-world fantastic! On the flip side, if you decide on something and that decision makes you feel less powerful, it's probably not the right choice. Napoleon Hill offered further insights in *Think and Grow Rich* about decision making:

> Analysis of several hundred people who had accumulated fortunes well beyond the million-dollar mark, disclosed the fact that *every one of them* had the habit of REACHING DECISIONS PROMPTLY, and of changing these decisions SLOWLY, if, and when they were changed. People who fail to

accumulate money, *without exception* have the habit of reaching decisions, IF AT ALL, very *slowly,* and of *changing these decisions quickly and often.*

⬤══════⬤

Part of the problem with making decisions in our current environment is that there's too much toxic and negative misinformation influencing us at all times. Advertisements, the news, social media, friends, family—everywhere we look, we're bombarded with opinions on what to do, where to go, and how to live. Napoleon Hill observed the same thing in his time, which led him to a fascinating correlation that he described in *Think and Grow Rich*:

> The majority of people who fail to accumulate money sufficient for their needs, are, generally easily influenced by the "opinions" of others. They permit the newspapers and the "gossiping" neighbors to do their "thinking" for them. "Opinions" are the cheapest commodities on earth. Everyone has a flock of opinions ready to be wished upon anyone who will accept them. If you are influenced by "opinions" when you reach DECISIONS, you will not succeed in any undertaking, much less in that of transmuting YOUR OWN DESIRE into money. If you are influenced by the opinions of others, you will have no DESIRE of your own. . . . You have a brain and mind of your own. USE IT, and reach your own decisions. If you need facts or information from other people, to enable you to reach decisions, as you probably will in many instances; acquire these facts or secure the information you need quietly, without disclosing your purpose.

⬤══════⬤

How to Make the Right Decision Every Single Time

One of the primary reasons why people don't make committed decisions is because they have doubts about whether they're making the right decision or not. Somehow they come to believe that making *no* choice is better than making *some* choice, and they wind up trapped in self-doubt. There are two key reasons why: (1) They're unable to trust themselves enough to make life-changing decisions, thus creating internal dissonance; and (2) they're unable to move forward because they've devalued their personal power; thus, they feel stuck.

First, let's define what the term *right decision* means. Basically, it's one that turns out well for you. For instance, if you're offered two jobs, the "right" decision would be choosing the one that gives you the most benefits, which include money, lifestyle demands, your overall happiness, and other factors.

And what are those other factors? Perhaps one job pays less, but the position allows you to more fully express your creativity. Or one has better pay, but it's a boring office job where you'd be stuck in a cubicle. If you were a robot and the choice was purely about the money, there's no issue here: take the higher pay. But you're *not* a robot, so your decision-making process is a lot more complicated, as evidenced by a 2017 Gallup study reporting that 85 percent of people worldwide hate their jobs. In the United States, comparatively speaking, only 70 percent of people hate their jobs—still a grim statistic.

We've been discussing raising your vibratory energy levels to get into the Zone. Well, it just so happens that this is the exact same process for making right decisions. Yes, it's that simple, and yet few people actually engage in it.

Using our example of having two job offers, take about fifteen or twenty minutes for meditation and deep breathing to get your vibrations flying high. Once you're in the Zone, focus on your job opportunities one at a time, and pay close attention to how you feel when you think of each. If one causes you to feel a drop in your energy, particularly if that takes the form of nausea or a tightness in your stomach area—in your body's emotional center—then it is definitely *not* the right choice for you! But if one offer causes you to feel elation and excitement, then it's definitely the right choice at this time.

It's likely you'll feel more excited about the job that allows you to fully express your creativity, even though it pays less. If you feel anxious about the money, put those worries aside and focus on staying in the Zone. You'll find that other ideas will come flowing in on how this position can still work out for you. For example, maybe you'll get a quick promotion because your creative talents will shine so brightly. Or perhaps you'll pick up some freelance assignments that you can do on the weekends. Remain open in the Zone to find a way to make the more desirable position work for you. Sometimes those ideas come instantly, and sometimes they take a while. Just be patient while Source Energy strings things together in the perfect order—but actively keep your energy as "high flying" as possible. Maintain keep your deep sense of *knowing* that everything happens in the quickest, highest, and best way for all involved.

Protect Your Energy As If Your Life Depends on It, Because Your Life Does Depend on It!

Once in a while someone will ask me, "Does all this 'energy-attraction' stuff really work the way you say? Because if it does, why does an innocent young child get raped or murdered when she doesn't have the awareness to attract anything but a godlike energy vibration?"

Well, I believe we come into this lifetime with past karma, which is nothing more than a vibrational energy sequence we've experienced in a past life, or many past lives, and that imprint comes with us into the new life we've been born into this time around. It's residual energy. For example, if you were a warrior in a past life, you'd carry some of that warrior energy into your current incarnation. If you were a victim of a horrible crime in a past life, then you'd carry some of that victim energy with you as well.

I also believe the karmic scales always balance themselves out. If you decided to hurt people and got away with it, this *residual low energy and vibration* will still follow you into your next life and, likely, for many lifetimes thereafter. This is why you must focus on raising your energy. It can help heal the pains of your past while protecting you from the clutches of low-vibrational people including rapists, robbers, and murderers. It can also protect your loved ones: your spouse, children, friends, pets, and others. Therefore, for your own sake and for the sake of those around you, practice keeping your vibrations sky-high!

Take the Ball and Run with It

Imagine a fluffy, playful puppy. Let's call him "Bundles." Now imagine that you're sitting outside with Bundles, but instead of engaging with him, you decide to read a book. He jumps on your lap, nibbles at your arm, and does all sorts of things to get your attention because he wants to play. But you don't *want* to play, so you just keep your nose stuck in that book. Eventually, he gives up and just sits there.

Now, if you look up from your book and tell Bundles to go fetch a ball, he'll run after it and come back ready for more. But let's say it was just a onetime shot for you—he fetches the ball, drops it at your feet, excitedly waits for you to toss it again, and you do nothing. Or worse, you get up and walk back into your home, ignoring the puppy and the ball. With no attention from you, Bundles will stop trying, and most likely slink away, sad and disappointed.

However, after he fetches the ball, drops it at your feet, excitedly waits for you to toss it again, and you engage in play, then Bundles becomes very active. He runs after the ball each time, brings it back to you, and brims over with joy, because you've been giving him attention.

Source Energy works in much the same way. If ideas are dropped at your feet and you decide not to do anything with them, Source

Energy will stop trying. It will take your non-engagement as a signal that you're just not that interested in pursuing the things you said you wanted, after all. Or perhaps you changed your mind. Either way, Source Energy isn't going to keep tugging at you for attention until you begin to put in motion the ideas and thoughts of inspiration that have already been given to you.

Source Energy *loves* action and motion because energy is motion, and motion is energy! The higher the energy, the faster the motion. The more quickly you implement the ideas and plans that are given to you, the faster your next action steps will be provided to you.

My daughter was playing a game app on her tablet called *Magic Piano*, where she'd have to use her fingertips to touch colored dots that would then play a well-known song. The faster the dots would come, the faster she'd have to react to make the music. The dots never stopped coming. In fact, the faster she went, the faster the dots reappeared in a never-ending loop. Source Energy works in the same way. The ideas, recommended plans of action, and resources will come to you continuously—that is, if you're responsive to what you're given. And that is the case even if the gift is only a first step in a yet-to-be-revealed complete plan.

Keep All Plans and Ideas to Yourself!

Have you ever heard about crabs in a bucket? As one of them manages to climb to the top of the pile, other crabs will pull him back down to the bottom. Unfortunately, there are low-thinking people who operate in the same way. Australians call this the Taller Poppy Syndrome: fellow mates will cut down to size a poppy plant when it grows taller than the other poppy plants in the hedge. This could be in the form of fame, fortune, or whatever a "taller poppy" looks like, in their view.

Unless you were fortunate enough to be born and raised, or currently reside, in a highly successful entrepreneurial household, the likelihood that you have positive, supportive entrepreneurial-minded people around you is unlikely. This means that there's a high risk that when you introduce some of your "grandiose visions" about how you see your life unfolding, naysayers will end up talking you out of going after your dreams. To be safe and protect your energy—at least for now—keep all your burning desires, goals, dreams, and plans to yourself.

Nobody likes dealing with people who drain our energy, waste our time, or cast dark clouds with their very presence. You know you're a target of such an individual if you feel a downward tug of depression, or the hair on the back of your neck stands up. You may start to feel angry or irritated. Or you may feel repulsed by this person's presence. As you start heightening your vibrations to connect with Source Energy, you'll more quickly and easily be able to separate low-vibe folks from high-vibe individuals. Going a step further, you'll understand that you'll need to routinely release low-vibe people from your life in order to gain significant traction.

This process could turn out to be a daily battle for you at first. After all, low-energy people like to suck high-energy people dry. This is because they've lost their own connection with Source Energy, so they try getting energy from some other immediately available source like you. Basically, they're energy vampires.

Commit to *fiercely protecting* your energy as if your life depends on it—and in many ways your life *does* depend on it. Within a short time, you'll become so powerful with your high-flying vibrational energy waves that even the most miserable, negative people will find your powerful energy vortex too much for them to deal with, and they'll move on to someone else and try to drain *their* energy instead. Or, being optimistic, if they *can* deal with your powerful energy vortex, then you might help bring them up. They can go from sadness and irritation to hopefulness and elation. You'll know you've mastered the attainment of a higher energy level when you can thwart all negativity, even when you intentionally expose yourself to it in the process of helping someone else.

Don't let yourself become discouraged if you find yourself attracting these naysayers, because you will also attract high-vibe people who are on the same frequency as you. We'll discuss attracting people more in a subsequent chapter.

The Separation of the Dark and the Light

More than twenty years ago, metaphysical and spiritual author Stuart Wilde wrote a book called *The Quickening*. He talked about how there's a change in speed at which things are evolving. It reminded me of Stephen King's *Dark Tower* books, where he wrote about "the thinning." Not only are things evolving much quicker than in generations before, but there's likely a collision of planes of existence causing our spiritual evolution to also move forward faster than ever.

I see this as part of a worldwide "cleaning house" period in which a spiritual energy movement is creating a clear distinction for each of us to decide: Do we want to be on the side of the dark or on the side of the light? Do we want to be aligned with the God Force and the Light, or not? Do we want to have an easier time while we're here on this earthly plane of existence, or not?

When you're aligned with Source Energy, your decision is easy and comforting, as you're confident that it will never send you down the wrong path. Your job—your *only* job—is to send out your request, listen and watch for ideas and thoughts of inspiration, and then implement those gifts by taking immediate action. The rest of what you'll need for your journey will follow. It really is that simple, so stop making it more difficult than it needs to be.

Chapter Nine

THE EIGHTH STEP TOWARD RICHES: PERSISTENCE AND YOUR FORCE OF WILL

Perseverance can overcome all obstacles. Even the laws of nature cannot stop it.

—JOHN D. ROCKEFELLER

Not too long ago I was very late getting to the airport for a flight out of Los Angeles. There had been a terrible accident on the freeway that made what should have been a ninety-minute morning rush-hour trip two and a half stressful hours long. This is when I discovered the power of *sheer force of will*. I knew that I'd have to figuratively part the seas to make the flight, so I did. I remember yelling out loud in my car, "How am I going to make this flight? Help me!"

I suddenly remembered that I had the contact information for a sky cab at the airport who could help me with my bags. I called, and a helpful man assured me that he'd be waiting for me. I then had the inspiration to get off at another exit. Sure enough, the traffic moved faster, and I made it to LAX, dropped off my bags, and then—as politely as I could—cut through four lanes of bumper-to-bumper traffic to get to the nearest parking garage.

When I got to the garage, there didn't seem to be any parking spaces anywhere. I was just one among many cruising the aisles for a space. In a combination of a *definite command* and *angry will*, I yelled out loud, "Help me find a parking spot!" Instantly and intuitively, I backed up, went down a different aisle, and immediately saw an empty parking spot next to a pillar. Plus, it was right next to the stairs to the terminal! I parked, ran in, politely cut through the line—with people's permission, of course—and made it just as the flight attendants were in the process of closing the boarding door. If I'd squandered another thirty seconds, I would have missed the flight. That's how close I was.

As I sat in my seat, sweating profusely and breathing heavily, I promised myself that I'd never let that happen again. *Never.* I hate being under that kind of extreme stress. Then I thought: *How the hell did I make this flight? And how can I more easily parlay that same magic into other areas of my life?*

I realized that the reason I wasn't satisfied in some parts of my life was because I allowed myself to be too timid in asking for the things I wanted while also allowing pesky sprinklings of doubt lead me to believe that what I wanted wasn't possible. I wasn't *commanding* what I wanted; I wasn't sending out a pure, unwavering and highly focused *sheer sense of will*. Source Energy can't help me (or you), if there's a lack confidence as far as where we want to go.

If it was okay for me to express my *unbridled force of will* when trying to catch a plane, then I realized that it was okay for me to do the same thing for more important things in my life. It made no sense to think otherwise. I had no time to sit around for days, weeks, months, or even years to give myself a list of reasons how to catch the flight; I was in the moment, *exerting my will* without making excuses or flaking out.

Since then, I've opened myself up to a whole new world of possibilities that I'd previously pushed aside because I thought they weren't doable or realistic. Realistic to whom? To me? To you? To somebody else?

When you're bold, persistent, and exert a force of will, this will separate you from the pack. Sending out indecisive energy with no real commitment is, in fact, making a decision to block assistance from Source Energy.

To use your sheer force of will is much different from willpower, though. Willpower implies forcing yourself to do something that isn't fun, like staying on a diet of carrots and celery all day when you're really craving a sandwich.

Sheer force of will means sending out a highly focused and powerfully projected energy field in the direction of your burning desire with very clear intent, refusing any other options. You are commanding that this *will* happen in one way or another, and you will accept nothing less, while remaining flexible on how Source Energy will unfold to help you get there. Having an open mind with respect to the multitudes of options on how to attain your goal is essential to getting what you want in the fastest and easiest way possible. You may believe your own plan is the highest and best, but it may not necessarily be how Source Energy manifests on a higher vibrational level.

Here's an experiment that you can do to practice exerting your force of will. The next time you're driving and see a car creeping out of an intersection with the intent of cutting you off, say "No!" and direct a laser-beamlike energy stream toward that person. You'll notice that the driver will stop doing what he was about to do instantly. It's almost as if he or she can hear you. Obviously that's not the case, but your force of will does travel through the ethers. As long as you *know* the driver will stop the moment you set forth your command, this is exactly what will occur. It works every time for me.

First, Get to the Core of What's Screwing You Up!

I conduct seminars, workshops, and special retreats several times a year. One particular event is intended for inner success, personal transformation, and wealth attraction, which starts with one main intent: getting to the *core* of what is holding back the participants from doing and having exactly what they want in their lives. For some, it's wealth beyond their wildest dreams. For others, it's a desire to find the perfect mate.

The core obstacle for people in any of life's four major quadrants—money, love, health, and family—is usually one or more significant experiences that took place during childhood. Uncovering your *core incident* is vital to the process of getting over it. Without knowing which part of your childhood self is interfering with steering your adult self, you'll continue to use it as a point of self-sabotage.

The exercise below requires a pad of paper and a pen. You should take a few moments for yourself, preferably someplace in nature like the woods or by the ocean, to dig deep for those painful experiences in your early life that made you feel insecure, unworthy, or unable to succeed.

Say to yourself: "What incident in my past is holding me back from the success and wealth I want in life? I'm ready to face the truth so that I can get past it for my new, brighter future."

Then just sit there. Enjoy the breeze on your face. Listen to the birds. Notice the flowers and trees. Appreciate nature. Completely *let go* of your thoughts. Pretty soon, you'll become aware of one experience in particular that has been most significant in holding you back in the present. There may be more than one core incident, but usually there's one particular event that started a domino effect.

Once you identify the core incident holding you back, write it down. But write it from the perspective of you as a child, who felt an initial sense of betrayal, inadequacy, trauma, or violation. It may look something like this: "When I was six years old . . ." Then describe your core incident. Continue with: "This made me feel . . ." Then write down your feelings. Conclude by writing as your current adult self: "I believe there's a connection between this childhood core incident and feeling held back in my adult life now because . . ." Then describe your revelations.

Take some deep breaths. You may find that even more memories come up that arose during or after that time in your childhood. Remember, you'll tend to "collect" memories that support the experience of that core incident, and reject those that do not, even if they make more sense. For example, if your core incident has to do with your mom taking money from your piggy bank and then lying about it, your core feeling behind this experience is likely to be *betrayal*. Therefore, *any* incident of betrayal thereafter would be collected as *support* for this core incident, while most positive incidents that oppose it would be rejected.

That is, if your mom came clean about taking the money from your piggy bank and explained that she wasn't thinking straight at the time because your dad had just lost his job, you may still not have forgiven her, even though doing so might have made sense. And if she later paid you back, plus a generous bonus to make up for her mistake in not asking you first, you still may have found that you'd lost trust in her, even though trusting her again might have made sense. She may have even spent the next several years trying to make up for her mistake by praising you for "helping out" the family when it was most needed at the time, but you unconsciously tend to reject all that while continuing to "collect" what corresponds to your feelings of betrayal.

It starts with the core incident, and then you pile into your emotional and mental storage vault whatever else supports an "I-told-you-so" argument with yourself about how everyone betrays you. You let the limited perception of yourself as a child dictate how you live your life now as an adult.

Whip Out the Pink Eraser, and Start Erasing the Past

I endured a painful breakup with someone I thought I was going to have a healthy and happy lifelong relationship with. I really struggled to deal with this because I knew I'd allowed myself to become too vulnerable, too soon. But I also knew that I had to overcome this situation quickly; otherwise, it would ruin how I felt for months and could even damage my perception of future relationships. As a result, I started telling myself, "I'd be okay right now if I'd never met him in the first place." And then I said, "What if I just erase it?"

The notion was ridiculous, right? However, each morning, night, and any other time I felt the pain bubbling up along with the memories I wanted to forget, I'd think of a large pink eraser. In my mind I'd begin to erase the things we did and the way I felt. I'd erase until I could see that the paper was clean, with only eraser residue crumbled all over it. Sometimes I'd erase so hard that the paper would appear to be ripped and torn apart.

I was changing my association of what I saw and felt about the relationship. Over a short period of time, I started feeling differently about this man. I even got to the point where I didn't need the mental vision of a big eraser and a piece of paper. Instead, whenever any painful feelings or memories came up, I'd say out loud, "Erase, erase, erase!" Pretty soon, all the hurtful feelings disappeared.

Of course, the memories are still there, but when I think about this man or the things we did together, I'm not at all attached to the relationship. The memories exist, but without the pain I had earlier associated them with.

I urge you to experiment with ways in which *you* can apply this technique to persistently let go, move forward, and get what you want in life.

Your Persistence and Your Dream

In *Think and Grow Rich*, Napoleon Hill was blunt about the meaning of *persistence*. He related this message in his story about singer Kate Smith and her deep desire to become successful on Broadway:

> For years she sang, without money, and without price, before any microphone she could reach. Broadway said to her, "Come and get it, if you can take it." She did take it until one happy day Broadway got tired and said, "Aw, what's the use? You don't know when you're whipped, so name your price, and go to work in earnest." Miss Smith named her price! It was

plenty. Away up in figures so high that one week's salary is far more than most people make in a whole year.

Verily it pays to be PERSISTENT!

And here is an encouraging statement which carries with it a suggestion of great significance—THOUSANDS OF SINGERS WHO EXCEL KATE SMITH ARE WALKING UP AND DOWN BROADWAY LOOKING FOR A "BREAK"—WITHOUT SUCCESS. Countless others have come and gone, many of them sang well enough, but they failed to make the grade because they lacked the courage to keep on keeping on, until Broadway became tired of turning them away.

Persistence is a state of mind, therefore it can be cultivated. Like all states of mind, persistence is based upon definite causes, among them these:

a. **DEFINITENESS OF PURPOSE.** Knowing what one wants is the first and, perhaps, the most important step toward the development of persistence. A strong motive forces one to surmount many difficulties.

b. **DESIRE.** It is comparatively easy to acquire and to maintain persistence in pursuing the object of intense desire.

c. **SELF-RELIANCE.** Belief in one's ability to carry out a plan encourages one to follow the plan through with persistence. (Self-reliance can be developed through the principle described in the chapter auto-suggestion.)

d. **DEFINITENESS OF PLANS.** Organized plans, even though they may be weak and entirely impractical, encourage persistence.

e. **ACCURATE KNOWLEDGE.** Knowing that one's plans are sound, based upon experience or observation, encourages persistence; "guessing" instead of "knowing" destroys persistence.

f. **CO-OPERATION.** Sympathy, understanding, and harmonious cooperation with others tend to develop persistence.

g. **WILLPOWER.** The habit of concentrating one's thoughts upon the building of plans for the attainment of a definite purpose, leads to persistence.

h. **HABIT.** Persistence is the direct result of habit. The mind absorbs and becomes a part of the daily experiences upon which it feeds. Fear, the worst of all enemies, can be effectively cured by <u>forced repetition of acts of courage</u>. Everyone who has seen active service in war knows this.

◈━━━◈

The only way to "cut through" resistance is to have the state of mind that you will not accept any result other than the manifestation of your burning desire. Your sheer sense of will can push aside any frivolousness, weakness, and extraneousness and bring into laser focus a *concrete decision* about what you want to do and who you want to be. Then, *go for it*—despite any fears, possibility of failure, and lack of know-how as far as how you'll get where you want to be!

In *Think and Grow Rich,* Napoleon Hill wrote about this very issue of rising above it all:

> The majority of people permit relatives, friends, and the public at large to so influence them that they cannot live their own lives, because they fear criticism.
>
> Huge numbers of people make mistakes in marriage, stand by the bargain, and go through life miserable and unhappy, because they fear criticism which may follow if they correct the mistake. This form of fear causes irreparable damage by destroying ambition, self-reliance, and the desire to achieve.
>
> Millions of people neglect to acquire belated educations, after having left school, because they fear criticism.
>
> Countless numbers of men and women, both young and old, permit relatives to wreck their lives in the name of DUTY, because they fear criticism. Duty can destroy personal ambitions and the right to live life in one's own way.

People refuse to take chances in business, because they fear the criticism that may follow if they fail. *The fear of criticism, in such cases is stronger than the DESIRE for success.*

⊱══╾══╼══⊰

Is the reason you do not follow your deepest desires because you fear what other people might say? Is this why you don't write that book, because of the possible one-star reviews? Is this why you don't delete your social media accounts, because people might think you buried yourself under a rock? Is this why you won't start a new business, because of the fear of ridicule from people around you if your enterprise fails?

For most of us, failure is really nothing more than a result we didn't expect or want. It's like going to the mall to find a red sweater but not finding one. So, instead, we settle on a white one. Technically, this could be construed as a "failure" because we set out with an intent to find a red sweater but instead got a different result. Yet, in actuality, finding our way to an alternative result isn't that bad of a deal, after all.

A lot of people fear the criticism they may receive if they get a different result than they planned on. As an example, starting a new business but ultimately not succeeding at it isn't usually devastating in and of itself. It's the whirlwind of negative comments from friends and family that stings the most.

Similarly, let's say a young man sets out to become a jazz musician only to find that no club will book him. He may find that it's the pity and judgment from those around him at the next holiday dinner that hurts so deeply. It isn't the failure that he's afraid of; it's the criticism *surrounding* the failure that is the most devastating.

Perhaps this is why I'm so successful in my many business enterprises. Actually, there are two reasons for this: (1) I don't have many personal friends or family members in my life who would be in a position to criticize me about anything; and (2) I just don't care what people think. This has allowed me to harness some amazing personal power.

If you want the same power for yourself, I suggest that you stop giving a damn about what people think and move into *fearless living*. Yes, that's right: start living fearlessly! Fear no one. Fear no situation. Fear no circumstance. Fear *nothing*. This alone will open new doors for you in ways you never imagined possible.

Chapter Ten

THE NINTH STEP TOWARD RICHES: BRINGING FORTH YOUR PERSONAL POWER

The Master Mind Principle: Two or more people actively engaged in the pursuit of a definite purpose with a positive mental attitude, constitute an unbeatable force.

—NAPOLEON HILL

When my third marriage wasn't working, I knew I had to make a decision. It took about five years of waffling back and forth before I decided that my husband and I needed to end things. In that moment of decision, I felt an instant feeling of freedom and relief. I felt like a one-ton weight had been removed from my shoulders, like I could finally breathe again. At that moment, I took back my personal power and decided to no longer put up with feeling like a victim of circumstance.

Many people who've been abused or who've had some other cataclysmic event take place in their lives often feel unable to move forward, stuck in a state of victimhood. They use a past incident—old or recent—as their victim calling card, the one they like to tell everybody about. Their story corroborates their sense of helplessness and inability to get anywhere in life. But their story is just that: a *story.*

No matter how traumatic any situation or circumstance was in your past, you're sitting here now, in a brand-new moment. You can choose to take this new moment to capture your personal power, grab the reins of your life, and steer yourself in the right direction. It is very much a conscious choice on your part, and you have nobody to blame but yourself if you choose to keep playing that old pity-party tune of hurt, anguish, and despair.

A fierce *power* is required to get what you want, no matter what it is. This power is found through aligning yourself with high-vibratory Source Energy, making definitive decisions about what you want, and then taking consistent action toward achieving it. It is also quite beneficial to surround yourself with a network of people and other resources who can help you fulfill your desires. But whatever the case, you must *know* that your burning desire has already been manifested and will reveal itself at the right time as your new destiny unfolds.

In *Think and Grow Rich*, Napoleon Hill described the value and benefits of personal power:

⬖═══⬗

PLANS are inert and useless, without sufficient POWER to translate them into ACTION. This chapter will describe the method by which an individual may attain and apply POWER . . . POWER IS REQUIRED FOR THE ACCUMULATION OF MONEY! POWER IS NECESSARY FOR THE RETENTION OF MONEY AFTER IT HAS BEEN ACCUMULATED!

Unfortunately, it's possible that your personal power was crushed at a very young age. You may have been told too many times: "No," "You can't," "You shouldn't," "Don't do that," "You're wrong," and perhaps worse. At some point, those messages became embedded in your subconscious mind, where they still live today. They reveal themselves in the form of you squeaking through life, expecting to be told or shown that you're limited in what you can do, and accepting less than the best for yourself.

On the bright side, you can break out of your limiting shell and expand your wings into limitless possibilities by simply harnessing your personal power again. You can go from walking on eggshells to *commanding* strength. Self-made movers and shakers are powerful people, and it's not because their station in life was handed to them. Many of these millionaires, billionaires, rock stars, and celebrities have a special aura about them. Their power forcefully emanates outward, which is why so many others tend to be attracted to them.

The way to emulate these individuals is to get into the flow. Connect with Source Energy. Bring your vibrational energy levels up, and keep them up for as long as you can. When you do so, you'll find yourself emanating brilliant energy out into the world. Others of like energy will be attracted to you in return, and many of these individuals can become part of your network to help you fulfill your burning desire and destiny.

Please know that there *is* power in numbers, and the faster you attract like-minded people into your realm of creation, the faster you'll be able to create what you want. For example, just a year ago I started making some pretty outrageous changes in my life. I started journaling three pages a day in the morning, and that seemed to open up a Pandora's Box of sorts. It helped me focus on what I *don't* want in my life anymore while allowing me to bring in what I *do* want to keep but perhaps modify a bit. By starting this three-page-a-day journaling practice, I also immediately opened up a new opportunity to raise my energy levels on a regular basis. Sometimes I use a morning meditation to accomplish this. Other times I listen to positive-thinking audios on YouTube while I journal. The goal is to elevate my energy for the day without aiming for a specific desire. All I do is raise my vibes with the sole intent of feeling better.

Within just a couple of months after I started engaging in this practice, all the people who were doing a disservice to me—including my *entire* office staff—ended up leaving for one reason or another. It was really a strange phenomenon. At the time, I was alarmed because I didn't understand what was going on. But once these people were swept out of my life like a fast-moving river, I found immediate solace in the arrival of a whole new group of individuals who were much more compatible with me. I realized that none of my old staff was at the level needed to keep up with my changing business, while my new team was instantly in alignment with the direction of my company. What was really amazing is that they all just showed up without me advertising, seeking them out, or even doing a single job interview! When you're ready for the change and you *let it happen*, it happens!

This is a perfect example if you're yearning for some kind of change but don't yet know what it looks like. By simply getting into the Zone with that high-flying vibrational state of being, the bad is swept away and the good sweeps in. Source Energy figures it all out for you. This includes sweeping out a bad relationship and sweeping in the person of your dreams; sweeping out a low-paying job with no advancement and sweeping in the perfect job with high pay, benefits, and tons of room for growth with the company; sweeping out your junker-clunker car and sweeping in a shiny new one. You get the point.

The key, as I've been telling you, is to just raise your energy level. That's it! Raise your energy and let the Universe work out some great things for you, especially if you're not quite sure in which direction you want to go. You'll find that some extraordinary things start happening in your life almost instantly!

The Secret Behind Three-Page-a-Day Journaling

First, I'd like to give credit where credit is due. I learned about the three-page-a-day journaling technique in a book by Julia Cameron called *The Artist's Way*. This is an excellent resource, and I recommend it to everyone.

There is great magic in journaling, in part because your mind can't always determine the difference between what has happened in your past, what you have in your present, and what you want to have in your future. Writing it all down helps you gain clarity so you can begin manifesting faster than you ever imagined.

You'll also notice that the *way* you journal changes as you proceed. You'll focus less on ranting and complaining and more on your intentions, positive thoughts, and gratitude. Regardless, let it all come up and out. Do *not* chastise yourself for having negative thoughts and beliefs. Instead, release them, and let your vibrational-energy output rise from low to high.

I write my three pages every morning, and since starting this practice, I've never missed a single day. *Never.* Sometimes my entries are about what I intend to accomplish that day or that week. For example, I may write: "I intend to do a thirty-minute weight-training workout every evening this week." On occasion, I write about what I intend to manifest, such as a new car, a new business, or a new relationship, which can lead to brainstorming creative ideas. I often express my profound gratitude for the wonderful life I already have, knowing that by acknowledging the awesomeness I've created so far, more awesomeness is on the way.

Other times, I listen to uplifting audio recordings and integrate that material into my writing. Every once in a while, I vent about something that's bothering me. In many instances, I find myself journaling about a project I'm working on, which leads to even more brainstorming. Or, I walk through my intentions as far as what I plan to accomplish that day. There's really no wrong or right way to keep a daily journal. Just do it, and do it consistently—three pages a day no matter what is going on in your life.

One positive result, in particular, has been an increase in my ability to confront disempowering beliefs head-on and replace them with empowering alternatives. For example, the moment I start thinking negatively, I dig deeper to understand why I'm feeling that way and then decide how I'm going to reframe that belief so I can start manifesting the things I want and stop manifesting the things I don't want.

What happens to my journal pages at the end of each entry? For the most part, I never read them again. Sometimes when I get a brilliant idea that I think I might want to go back to, I'll put a sticky note on the page and draw a star next to the specific passage. What's more likely, though, is that I keep whipping through one journal after another and continue to move forward. When I've filled up a journal, I'll write the start and finish dates on the front cover, then park it on my bookshelf.

One last thing I'd like to mention is that some people just hate writing and therefore find journaling to be very difficult. If this is the case for you, you might find it more useful to keep a sketchbook instead. You can doodle on your daily pages instead of writing on them. Or perhaps you'd rather keep a gratitude journal instead, writing down all the things you're grateful for that happened during the day, and that you *intend* to see happen in the near future. Or maybe you'd like to keep a hybrid writing-doodle-gratitude journal. Just do what you need to do to stick to this powerful and healing daily practice. The most important thing is that it has to be comfortable, fun, and just right for *you*.

Journaling is life changing, so run out and get your journal so you can start writing. Go! Do it right now! I'll wait!

The Power of Like-Minded and Like-Energy People Coming Together

Mastermind groups were originated for the purpose of connecting the world's most powerful people to advance their businesses and investments. They understood the true power of their alliances and still, to this day, continue to build them to enhance their wealth. Unfortunately, everyday people like you and me aren't usually invited in, so we've taken to forming our own groups to share thoughts, ideas, and inspiration. In a well-formed group, you and other like-minded people can co-create a sense of magic when brainstorming ideas and plans. Napoleon Hill, in *Think and Grow Rich*, described this as a "psychic" experience:

> Keep in mind the fact that there are only two known elements in the whole universe, energy and matter. It is a well-known fact that matter may be broken down into units

of molecules, atoms, and electrons. There are units of matter which may be isolated, separated, and analyzed. Likewise, there are units of energy. The human mind is a form of energy, a part of it being spiritual in nature. When the minds of two people are coordinated in a SPIRIT OF HARMONY, the spiritual units of energy of each mind form an affinity, which constitutes the "psychic" phase of the Master Mind.

Hill talked about some of his "invisible friends," who could be described as an imaginary mastermind group consisting of "major players" in history such as Abraham Lincoln. At first, I thought it was the stupidest thing ever to pretend through meditation that you're in a room with certain people who would be best qualified to give guidance in certain areas of your life. Then I tried it—and I was dumbfounded by the results. The ideas given to me by "talking" to these "mentors" as if they were right in front of me were astounding.

Several decades ago, after my grandmother had passed, I found that I had the gift to talk to people on the Other Side. Since then, I've been able to connect with the deceased—usually without my direct control—and I've met all kinds of individuals.

It was only recently that I started reeling in this gift and pinpointing specific souls I wanted to meet with "over there." That's when I decided I wanted to know what Napoleon Hill thought of this book you're reading—that is, if he thought I was stepping on his ghostly toes by publishing a work based on his writings, and if he approved of what I was doing. Weeks went by, and I still didn't "see" Hill. Then a few days before I was to meet Bill Gladstone, the agent helping me bring this book to the world, I saw Napoleon Hill in a dream. It was on his birthday, October 26, to be exact. He was smiling ear to ear, giving me a thumbs-up on my book. He added, "Be sure to put in a lot of carets."

When I woke up that morning, I tried to figure out what he'd told me. I heard him say "carets," which sounds the same as "carrots" or "carats." But I knew what he meant. In the publishing world, a caret is an editorial arrowhead-like symbol like this (^), used to indicate where to insert punctuation or words. Now, of course, we have computers, so insertions are implemented in the moment, and the old carets aren't used much unless you write and edit by hand. Back in Hill's time, though, he would draw a caret between two words and then handwrite his added word or an entire sentence above it. Having studied his original manuscripts, I found that he frequently used carets in his manuscript drafts.

Knowing that he gave his full approval from the Other Side and even offered suggestions on how to make this book better—not to mention the mysterious arrival of the Lost Chapters of *Think and Grow Rich* arriving mysteriously at my doorstep—was a great relief. Without Hill's validation, this book would not be in your hands right now. I'm particularly grateful for his guidance in adding my thoughts and ideas to his work with the intent of communicating in a way accessible to today's readers, including the references to technology and modern science, which didn't exist during his time on Earth. This entire process has been an incredible experience. Much of what I write here is inspired by feeling Napoleon Hill's presence and knowing that he is my "coauthor."

You may or may not feel comfortable imagining yourself in the company of powerful people—*out of body or alive*—to allow yourself to open up to thoughts of inspiration and guidance. If you don't, you can still help yourself facilitate workable steps toward attaining your burning desire just by "feeling" your way through the process on your own.

If you want to form a *real* mastermind group with real people in it, make sure that it's for the purpose of serving one vision, and it's made up of individuals who are on the same high-wavelength energy level that you're on.

My mastermind group is my staff. I make sure to surround myself with people who match the vibrational levels I want to maintain during my workday. There's nothing worse than surrounding yourself with negative individuals while you're trying to be productive and action oriented.

But if you work at a job where you don't get to call the shots and there are all kinds of negative, low-vibe people around you, it's *your* responsibility to bring up your own energy levels. The others will either choose to bring up their energy to be in your realm or they'll choose to disappear from your immediate environment.

Think about it this way: You're probably aware that you carry yourself differently when you're in the presence of someone who is well dressed and polished versus someone who is sloppy and rude. That is an example of your energy levels vibing up or vibing down.

Lifting Others Up Through Service

When you emit high vibratory energy, you never feel the need to judge others. If low-vibe people are in your orbit, you can still keep high-vibing without judgments about what they should do to get their lives together. That's none of your business. This acknowledgment alone will bring up the energy levels of those around you.

Being in service to others with a meaningful product or service is another way to lift up other people's energy levels—for example, helping others get what they want in all areas of life. There is a big demand for this service. Plus, the more people you help to get what they want, the richer *you* will become.

Creating inspired art, music, literature, and entertainment is another way to share your higher vibrational level with others. These creations are in their purest form and are manifested for the purpose of enlightening.

You know your service is in alignment with Source Energy if you feel absolutely fantastic when you think about it. Don't talk yourself out of it or tell yourself that it's too late or it's not possible. Don't defeat or deflate yourself. Just begin tapping into Source Energy, and more answers will come, my friend. The answers *always* come.

No matter what you decide on, do it out of a high vibratory state of being. Do it out of love. Do it out of service. If you live your life with this pure intent of soul and spirit, you'll *always* be taken care of by Source Energy.

Think Big!

At the same time you begin expanding your energy through your daily high-vibe exercises, you'll also expand your expectations of what you want in life. While you may have been satisfied with working in a cubicle over the past decade, you'll find that once you begin expanding your energy, the New You will push up against that cubicle looking for a way out. This may be concerning or uncomfortable to you at first, but rest assured, it's just the Universe saying, "Time to dream bigger now to match your bigger energy."

I love getting to this part of the journey. It's like being a kid in a candy store, where all possibilities suddenly open up. The things you never thought were possible before—or weren't even on your radar—now become certainties for you. Imagine dusting off those dreams of whatever it was you always wanted to be, or whatever it is that you *now* want to be, and seeing those dreams manifest into a reality like greased lightning! Yes, my friend, this is definitely on the horizon for you by simply shifting into success consciousness while increasing vibrational energy levels as much as possible.

Banish all doubt. Go big! Keep your inner knowing that everything will unfold in the perfect way as you go along. Know that your big dream will happen. *Feel* that it will happen. That's why you're here in the first place—to make your big dream happen!

"But It Takes Work to Keep My Vibes Up All the Time!"

In the beginning, it will take some focus and conscious effort to keep your vibrational energy up where it needs to be. Since you may have been a low- or medium-vibe person for many years, your brain pathways are conditioned to subconsciously remain at those levels. This means it may seem like a monumental effort to get to, and stay in, the Zone for long periods of time, but in about thirty days, your brain will begin to "rewire." Keep working at bringing up and sustaining your energy at these high-vibe levels, and pretty soon it will become second nature.

It's helpful to change certain elements of your diet as you're engaged in this process. You may wish to add organic foods, especially fruits and vegetables, to your daily regimen. I've found that cutting carbs and sugar out of my diet has helped stabilize my moods, which, in turn, helps keep my vibes high. I also limit alcohol and don't dabble in drugs at all. Both of these practices are known to drag down a person's vibrational energy.

Exercise is a great way to clear your mind and increase endorphins, which is akin to high vibes. If you're ever feeling blue, take a walk in the sun—the vitamin D generated in your body will thwart any depression you may be experiencing. Plus, a blast of serotonin and norphenlyephrine will flood through your body—the natural nemesis to the blues—after about thirty to forty-five minutes of exercise, making you feel great and putting you into a higher-vibrational state of being.

I've noticed that the reason why many people turn to drugs and alcohol is because they want that feeling of bliss, nirvana, and an elevated state of being. But those substances actually lower your vibrational field of energy while depleting your body of vital nutrients needed to feel balanced. By getting yourself into the Zone, you'll feel much more "high" than you'll ever feel with drugs or alcohol. So, as they say . . . just say no to drugs!

Chapter Eleven

THE TENTH STEP TOWARD RICHES: HOW TO USE SEX TRANSMUTATION TO ATTAIN YOUR DEEPEST DESIRES

Everything in life is about sex, except sex. Sex is about power.

—OSCAR WILDE

When you raise your energy level to attract the things you want, in many cases you'll find yourself pushing the energy upward from your base chakra through your body to get yourself into the Zone. It's in the Zone where you can revel in pure bliss, happiness, joy, and harmony while simultaneously manifesting everything you want: relationships, trips around the world, financial abundance, and more. Napoleon Hill's *secret of sex transmutation* is about applying the energy of your sexual desire to get what you want. He elaborated on this in *Think and Grow Rich*:

> Sex transmutation is simple and easily explained. It means the switching of the mind from thoughts of physical expression, to thoughts of some other nature.
>
> Sex desire is the most powerful of human desires. When driven by this desire, men develop keenness of imagination, courage, will-power, persistence, and creative ability unknown to them at other times. So strong and impelling is the desire for sexual contact that men freely run the risk of

life and reputation to indulge it. When harnessed, and redirected along other lines, this motivating force maintains all of its attributes of keenness of imagination, courage, etc., which may be used as powerful creative forces in literature, art, or in any other profession or calling, including, of course, the accumulation of riches.

◈══ ═══ ══◈

The Secret Behind Sex Transmutation That Was Never Revealed in Think and Grow Rich

Since sexuality is a powerful energy easily experienced by most people, channeling this energy at its peak at the same time you're summoning your burning desire is, quite possibly, the fastest way to attract what you want. The act of self-pleasure is the best way to do so, so you can focus on channeling this powerful and pleasurable *feeling state* to get what you want. This approach is particularly helpful if you find it difficult to practice daily meditation and visualization exercises.

Because the only language the Universe understands is that of feelings, when words are spoken, it "hears" the feelings behind them. This helps explain why you don't get what you want when you say, "I want this!" but deep down inside you believe, "I don't think I'm worthy of this." Naturally, the Universe complies with your order: in this case, "Hold up on the delivery because I'm unworthy."

What is so powerful about sexual energy is that you can get in this feeling state through unbridled pleasure, whereas during meditation, you may find that your mind wanders as you attempt to focus on your burning desire. Or, when trying to visualize your burning desire, you may find yourself engaged in self-doubt.

When you're in the midst of this passionate energy at the peak of an orgasm, your sexual energy is vibrating at such an intense level that it automatically pushes out distractions, doubts, or other resistance, and rewards you. It allows you to *feel*, and thus emanate an absolute *knowing* that your burning desire is already manifested and waiting for you to claim it. Think about this: the lead-up to the climactic moment is a focused, ultrapowerful feeling, which is what you also need in order to manifest whatever your burning desire is. So, you might as well parlay this to your advantage by focusing on your burning desire during your climax!

Although Napoleon Hill never admitted it, probably because of the strict morality of his time, I truly believe he was talking about tapping into this sexual power through orgasm. Instead, he wrote with more nuance in *Think and Grow Rich*:

> The creative imagination functions best when the mind is vibrating at an exceedingly high rate. That is, when the mind is functioning at a rate of vibration higher than that of ordinary, normal thought.
>
> When brain action has been stimulated, through one or more of the ten mind stimulants, it has the effect of lifting the individual far above the horizon of ordinary thought, and permits him to envision distance, scope, and quality of THOUGHTS not available on the lower plan, such as that occupied while one is engaged in the solution of the problems of business and professional routine.
>
> When lifted to this higher level of thought through any form of mind stimulation, an individual occupies, relatively, the same position as one who has ascended in an airplane to a heights from which he may see over and beyond the horizon line which limits his vision, while on the ground. Moreover, whole on this higher level of thought, the individual is not hampered or bound by any of the stimuli which circumscribe and limit his vision while wrestling with the problems of gaining the three basic necessities of food, clothing, and shelter. He is in a world of thought in which the ORDINARY, work-a-day thoughts have been as effectively removed as are the hills and valleys and other limitations of physical vision, when he rises in an airplane.

◆━━◆

How to Harness the Power of Sexual Energy for Your Manifestations

During most acts of self-pleasure, the focal point is a feeling of lust disconnected from any resistance. The key is to shift the paradigm from lustful sexual energy to pure energy directed toward what you want.

Sexual energy is very powerful. Of all the kinds of energy you could ever have, sexual energy is the most powerful because of the pure, focused, passionate result. When you choose to use this energy for manifestation, make sure that whatever you're focusing on is really what you wish to manifest. Because it isn't *necessarily* going to deliver the highest and best good; it's just going to deliver. So you have to be very sure and very careful when harnessing sexual energy.

In comparison, when you use regular meditation, visualization, and deep breathing to get into a high vibrational state, and then focus on your burning desire, the Universe responds safely, always bringing you your highest and best good.

What this means is that sexual energy can be used for both summoning beauty and wisdom and also for summoning demons. This is why you *must* use extreme caution when using it to fulfill your desires.

My advice to you is simple: Use your direct connection with Source Energy by getting into those high vibrational levels the conventional way—through meditation and deep breathing for fifteen to twenty minutes while also focusing on your burning desire. The Universe will then give you action steps to take while it aligns with the rest of your manifestation path. Once you know what those action steps are—including a very clear idea of what your burning desire is—then you can use sexual energy, with extreme caution, to move you farther along your path. In this way, you'll know *exactly* what it is you're going after and what you need to do to attain it. Your path will be based on pure ideas given to you directly from Source Energy. Relying on the limitations of your own mind to come up with what you *think* is best, and then using sexual energy for its manifestation is too risky—for me, anyway.

Now that I understand the power of sexual energy for the purposes of manifestation and creation, I find that I don't like to use it. Unless I'm 100 percent spot-on with a precise manifestation focal point and burning desire, I realize I may get something I don't want at all. Or, it may be something I *thought* I wanted, but when it arrives, I realize it's not for my highest or best good.

My intention, always, is for the highest and best good *for all*. This is why I stick with the traditional route of getting into the Zone by no longer choosing to take this sexual shortcut.

Chapter Twelve

THE ELEVENTH STEP TOWARD RICHES: GETTING YOUR SUBCONSCIOUS MIND TO WORK FOR YOU

Whatever we plant in our subconscious mind and nourish with repetition and emotion will one day become a reality.

—EARL NIGHTINGALE

My mom was disappointed in me when the dentist said my mouth was full of cavities. I was only seven or eight years old back then, but I already knew I was more disappointed in myself than she could ever be. I vowed that I'd never get a cavity again. And I never did—that is, until I was in my late thirties and mistakenly told myself, *Well, by this age, I'd certainly expect to have a cavity or two. Everybody else does, right?*

Sure enough, the very next dental checkup revealed that I had one cavity and the early start of another. I was so mad at myself. Why did I switch the script and consciously *decide* to have a cavity? I knew it was a creation of my own mind. The solution? Switch the script back. So I immediately told myself: *No more cavities for me.* And I haven't had one since.

This is an example of a very conscious awareness of a belief. But what about all those other beliefs in your subconscious mind? For example, in the past, when I knew I needed a break from work but wouldn't allow myself to take time off, I'd manifest a cold or flu to force a respite. Now I get as much rest as I need, and I rarely get sick. In fact, when everyone around me is sneezing and coughing, I'll simply affirm, "I have an amazing immune system, and I stay healthy." And I do.

In *Think and Grow Rich*, Napoleon Hill applied this same reasoning:

> THE SUBCONSCIOUS MIND WORKS DAY AND NIGHT. Through a method of procedure, unknown to man, the subconscious mind draws upon the forces of Infinite Intelligence for the power with which it voluntarily transmutes one's desires into their physical equivalent, making use, always of the most practical media by which this end may be accomplished.
>
> You cannot entirely control your subconscious mind, but you can voluntarily hand over to it any plan, desire, or purpose which you wish transformed into concrete form. . . . There is plenty of evidence to support the belief that the subconscious mind is the connecting link between the finite mind of man and Infinite Intelligence. It is the intermediary through which one may draw up on the forces of Infinite Intelligence at will. It, alone, contains the secret process by which mental impulses are modified and changed into their spiritual equivalent. It, alone, is the medium through which prayer may be transmitted to the source capable of answering prayer.

❖═══❖

An Easy Way to Circumvent Negative Beliefs

It's a lot of work to unravel a lifetime of negative and disempowering beliefs. And the older you are, the more unraveling there is to do. But here's the good news: raising your energy level is a better way to accomplish the same result *without* having to unravel your past.

When you raise your vibrational energy, you can immediately discern between what feels good and what feels rotten. When you're basking in the light of a high, pure vibe, anything that doesn't align with your energy wavelength will begin to pull you down. You'll know it because it will feel like rain clouds moving into your sunny skies. That moment of self-awareness is an opening to push those clouds away.

Earlier I wrote that high-vibe and low-vibe energy *cannot* coexist in the same space at the same time, and there are no exceptions to this law of quantum physics. What this means with respect to positive beliefs is that when you feel out-of-this-world extraordinary with your vibes flying high, you cannot entertain negativity in the form of disempowering or disparaging self-talk. It's just not possible.

As an example, for the longest time I had a belief about my unworthiness that worked its way through all aspects of my life, including my personal relationships with men. My first husband turned out to be abusive after we got married. The signs were there when we were dating, but being young and foolish, I didn't pay attention to them. I drew this kind of man into my life because of my core belief about my unworthiness.

The second man I attracted wasn't abusive. This is because I had *consciously decided* that I'd never have an abusive man in my life again. I even affirmed this in the strongest terms: "I will *never* have an abusive man in my life ever again." I'm happy to say that this decree has stood strong from that moment on and up until this very day. However, I didn't know that there were other things I should have also affirmed.

My second marriage was to a man who was a lazy deadbeat. Yes, I saw the signs beforehand, but I didn't acknowledge them until it was too late. For the sake of my two-year-old daughter, I ended the marriage. I did so because I knew that children adopt beliefs based on what they see and not what solely on what their parents tell them. I didn't want my daughter to come to believe that it's okay for the mom of the household to work day and night while the lazy dad does next to nothing. This experience led me to change my decree: "I will *never* have an abusive man or a lazy deadbeat man in my life ever again." I thought I had my bases covered, but apparently not.

I got married a third time. (Yes, I know, the madness just doesn't seem to end.) I got it right on my two pronouncements: he wasn't abusive, and he wasn't a deadbeat. But given my history of disempowering relationships, I wasn't in a state of trust with this man. We met at an event, hit it off, and when we got married, we both held the idea that "love conquers all" and "where there's a will, there's a way," but without mutual clarity on what that really meant. While I had the best of intentions and could have moved mountains with the intent I had to make the relationship work, he petered out, with his only enthusiasm about the marriage related to the financial benefits he reaped while being married to me.

It is critical that you're on the *same vibrational wavelength* as the other significant people in your life. When you're flying together with high vibes, Source Energy sends you synchronistic action steps for the benefit of your relationship. Otherwise, your best-laid plans, together or individually, will likely fall apart.

Perhaps the most powerful lesson I learned from these three marriages is that there's no such thing as a "failed" relationship. When one or both individuals grow in different directions, it can be empowering to move on without each other. Some have judged me harshly because I've been married and divorced three times. I even judged myself until I realized that I would have failed *me* had I stuck it out with any one of these men. I would have stunted my growth as a spiritual being, remaining in a box of misery and never spreading my wings in the way I'm doing right now.

For anyone who takes the vow "till death do us part," literally by believing they must stay in the marriage no matter what, death may come faster than you anticipate. By being in a loveless, soul-less marriage or relationship, you may be killing your spirit and your body with all the stress, anxiety, and depression. If children are involved, that can potentially make it worse for all involved. Maybe it's time to ask yourself if sacrificing your soul and who you are is worth staying in a disempowering relationship. The way

I see it, the rough patch from ending a disabling relationship is temporary compared to the lifelong gift and excitement of living up to your fullest potential.

Through my daily journaling, I've come to powerful realizations about patterns in the men I've been in relationships with: the most glaring one is that they all had weak or nonexistent relationships with their fathers. My first husband's dad had abandoned his family. My second husband's father had left when he was only two years old. My third husband's dad had taken his own life. The reason I attracted these men was because of my very weak relationship with my own father.

So now I have a new decree: "I will *never* be in a relationship of any kind with a man who is abusive in any way; who is a lazy, broke deadbeat; who is physically, mentally, or emotionally unavailable; or who has a weak, poor, or nonexistent relationship with his father." There! I think I've covered it all! I'm raising my energy level now, knowing that only the right man will arrive, and all others not in service of my best and highest good will fall away.

Resistance to anything is how you can sink your dream ship pretty fast. It makes it difficult to create new beliefs and develop an inner knowing that good things will manifest if you've had enough life experiences that made you cynical, pessimistic, and negative.

To give you an example, because my relationships haven't been so great, I've experienced *resistance* in accepting that a perfect mate will come into my life. Recognizing this state of resistance for what it is, I have to *shift away* from trying to visualize a literal representation of the perfect relationship and *shift into feeling* what the perfect relationship for me would be like. While some women may make a list of all the perfect qualities their ideal man may have, I've found great resistance in going this route myself. The very moment I begin to jot down this "Christmas list" of the perfect man, I get that pit in the bottom of my stomach. That's the resistance I'm talking about.

The key to visualization and to getting into that feeling state of what you desire is to find a way to *banish all resistance* to your dream. If you don't, you'll find that your dream will be withheld from you until you release this block once and for all.

I now find that I only have one requirement in a man: he must be the wind beneath my wings. And that's it. There's no list. Just that one thing. But here's the real kicker: I've gotten so high in my vibrational energy levels by being in the Zone that I realize I already *have* the wind beneath my wings—that is, *myself*!

If you think about it, it's the *feeling* of getting what we want that's the real goal anyway, right? If you want loads of cash, it's the *feeling* you'll get by having it and by being able to spend the money on whatever you want. If you want to lose weight, it's the *feeling* of confidence, personal self-esteem, and energy you'll have by reaching your ideal weight. If you want a perfect relationship, it's the *feeling* about being with someone who can provide you with a sense of security, happiness, and satisfaction.

But what if you can access that feeling *before* you attain any of your desires? Isn't that what you're really after to begin with? That is, the *feeling* of getting that desire—and not really the desire itself? By getting yourself into the Zone, your body, mind, and spirit will feel as if you've already manifested your desire. While this, in and of itself, could give you enough satisfaction, don't worry. The feeling state is the first place you need to get to before the desire will manifest. But it's nice to know that you'll feel pretty damn good while you're awaiting your goodies.

It's Not What You Ask for, It's How You Ask for It

One of the things I like to do in my journaling or when saying affirmations out loud is to ask Source Energy a question and receive an answer. For instance, if I've got a problem and I need an immediate solution, I ask, knowing that I will get a response.

How you ask your questions, though, is critical. Disempowering ones yield useless answers. For example, what if you asked,

"Why am I broke all the time?" It's a pretty silly question, if you think about it. Not only is it disempowering, but the answer won't enhance your prosperity. Here's some much better phrasing: "What can I do to generate net profits of $20,000 each month for myself?" This question is empowering, specific, and implies a *knowing* that the solution has already been manifested. Then let it go as Source Energy lines up a powerful and specific answer about career, business, or investments to arrive when the time is right.

In *Think and Grow Rich,* Napoleon Hill described the process of asking and receiving in this way:

> Everything which man creates, BEGINS in the form of a thought impulse. Man can create nothing which he does not first conceive in THOUGHT. Through the aid of the imagination, thought impulses may be assembled into plans. The imagination, when under control, may be used for the creation of plans or purposes that lead to success in one's chosen occupation.
>
> All thought impulses, intended for transmutation into their physical equivalent, voluntarily planted in the subconscious mind, must pass through the imagination, and be mixed with faith. The "mixing" of faith with a plan, or purpose, intended for submission to the subconscious mind, may be done ONLY through the imagination.
>
> ***Positive and negative emotions cannot occupy the mind at the same time.*** One or the other must dominate. It is your responsibility to make sure that positive emotions constitute the dominating influence of your mind. Here the law of HABIT will come to your aid. *Form the habit* of applying and using the positive emotions! Eventually, they will dominate your mind so completely, that the negatives cannot enter it.
>
> Only by following these instructions literally, and continuously, can you gain control over your subconscious mind. The presence of a single negative in your conscious mind is sufficient to *destroy* all chances of constructive aid from your subconscious mind.

When affirming, commanding, praying, or whatever it is you do to ask Source Energy to help you out, always make sure that your feelings are going to attract an exact vibrational match. If you emit a feeling of negativity despite the words you state, you'll receive back its negative equivalent. If you emit a feeling of positivity, you'll receive back its positive equivalent.

Gifting: A Technique for Increasing Vibrational Input

Anytime you begrudgingly jam your hand into your pocket to give someone money as a gift—regardless of whom the recipient is—stop yourself. If the feeling state of joy isn't there, then don't give it. Wait until your heart is on board for the gift to matter on a vibratory energy level. Money is energy. As with all energy, the intent and feeling behind it really counts. When you feel your heart brighten and expand upon giving a gift, you know you're in the right feeling state. It's the same one that also allows your gift to come back to you tenfold, a hundredfold, and sometimes much more.

When I give money, I automatically place trust in the Universe that there's much more to come. And I'm always right in that regard. More *always* comes. My abundance is never ending. In fact, the more I give, the more I get back—many times over!

The same applies to you, even if you don't realize it yet. So, make a conscious decision to constantly emanate high-energy vibes that always keep your channel with Source Energy wide open. As long as you do so, all your needs will be taken care of. Trust that this will be true for you . . . and it always will be.

Chapter Thirteen

THE TWELFTH STEP TOWARD RICHES: HOW THE BRAIN RECEIVES IDEAS AND INSPIRATION

....

Everything you want is downstream . . . just let go of the oars and the current will carry you.

—ABRAHAM-HICKS

....

Often in the wee hours of the morning—usually in between deep sleep and being half-wake—I'll hear songs in my head. They're not melodies swirling around inside my mind stemming from the last time I listened to the radio. They're songs I've *never even heard before*. If I were a musician or songwriter, I'd keep a tape recorder by my bedside and record them. I'm sure I'd be prolific too—that is, if songwriting were my burning passion. You see, Taylor Swift, Lady Gaga, and I share a secret.

It's a secret that *you* can get in on too: Creative talents, ideas, and inspirations are available to absolutely everyone at all times! Those able to be open to them while being in the Zone can receive an endless bounty of inventiveness. However, those who believe they don't have what it takes are simply shut off from this pipeline, but all they have to do is *flip a switch* to have access to this magical portal. Napoleon Hill wrote about this process in *Think and Grow Rich*:

Though the medium of the ether, in a fashion similar to that employed by the radio broadcasting principle, every human brain is capable of picking up vibrations of thought which are being released by other brains.

When stimulated, or "stepped up" to a high rate of vibration, the mind becomes more receptive to the vibration of thought which reaches it through the ether from outside sources. This "stepping up" process takes place through the positive emotions, or the negative emotions. Through the emotions, the vibrations of thought may be increased.

Vibrations of an exceedingly high rate are the only vibrations picked up and carried, by the ether, from one brain to another. Thought is energy traveling at an exceedingly high rate of vibration. Thought, which has been modified or "stepped up" by any of the major emotions, vibrates at a much higher rate than ordinary thought, and it is this type of thought which passes from one brain to another, through the broadcasting machinery of the human brain.

◈══════◈

Your mind can serve as a receptor of creativity, ideas, and inspiration once you understand how to "set it up."

As a very young child, I remember practicing ESP with my brother. I'd send him picture messages with my mind and ask him to tell me what I was thinking about. When he was focused and open, he was accurate every single time, and he wasn't even three years old back then.

That's how powerful the human mind can be. You can communicate through Infinite Intelligence without even opening your mouth. This channel can transmit over distances of millions of light-years in outer space and through concrete, steel, mountains, and jungles here on Earth. As remarkable as this is, it's not foolproof—simply transmitting what you want isn't good enough to *actually get* what you want. What you must do is clearly visualize and deeply feel what you want. The secret is not to pretend; it's to know that when your vibrations are flying high in the Zone, all things are possible.

The Nova

I need to start by saying that I'm not really a Steven Tyler or Aerosmith fan and know next to nothing about the band or their music. But on December 15, 2018, I had the most incredible dream:

> *My daughter and I, and a handful of others, were at Steven Tyler's house for a week-long Aerosmith "rock-star camp." Although I was glad to be there, I knew that making music wasn't my thing. I let Steven know that my daughter and I were going on a Disney cruise instead, but that we'd be back in time for his camp's wrap-up session. He answered with something like: "Too bad that you won't experience this with everyone else, so I'll tell you about my secret to success right now." Then he started talking about tapping into a place that he called the Nova.*
>
> *This place—the very center of the highest and most blissful point in life—was where he said anyone can experience a direct connection to art, music, science, inventions, and other amazing and powerful gifts. He said that this is where he finds inspiration for the music he writes, and for a lot of other things too. But to be able to get to this place, he said, "You must absolutely know, without a doubt, what your life purpose is." He went on to explain that knowing your life purpose and reveling in it means that you don't extract inspiration from the Nova, but rather, you align your destiny with it.*

When I woke up that morning, I had some revelations about the Nova. I understood it to be a *state of being* where there is a focused and unequivocal connection—without any doubt, fear, sense of confusion, or distraction—to a higher power. Steven Tyler wasn't coming from a place of, "Yeah, man, this song is going to make me rich and famous." He was in it for the magical, direct connection to this higher source by honoring his destiny.

I discovered long after I had that dream, in doing some follow-up research, that he'd in an interview that he was only able to reach the Nova when he was stoned or drunk—or both. At least at first. During that interview, he talked about when he was young and started his first band. Then suddenly he didn't have a band anymore and thought his dream to be a rock star was over. But something inside spoke to him about what he needed to do: "I knew in my heart that if I had a bro in the band like Mick [Jagger] had Keith [Richards], like the Kinks, you know, Dave and Ray; in any of those bands, where there were two guys that were tight and fed off each other." That's when he found Joe Perry, who would become the lead guitarist and founding member of Aerosmith.

Tyler's inner knowing guided him to that "band bro thing," and the Universe delivered Joe. About songwriting together, Tyler said, "Stuff would come out of my head while I was [doped up] . . . like '*sweeeeeet emotion.*' Wait, fuck! Get me a paper and pen! I'd write that shit down. Suddenly, whoops! The song ended up on the radio. See, so I used *that place* [the Nova] . . . for every song you've ever heard. '*Sweet Emotion*'—every one of those licks—'*Walk This Way*' . . . there's twenty that got lost in the ether."

Later on in life, Tyler was able to tap into the Nova without needing drugs or alcohol. About that, he said, "The best part of it is, when I got sober, I started writing even better shit. I'd go in a room with four guys and say, 'We're going in to write a hit. We're going to stay in this room until we fucking do or until we can't stand each other's smell.' And we'd leave in seven hours with a fucking song. And a good one. And one that would live way past all of us."

That was an ideal mastermind group: people who were 100 percent focused on a *single vision*, who were hyperfocused on that one vision, and who could get into that magical state of mind together to create synchronicity and alignment with Source Energy.

When your life is *on purpose*, moving in the same direction as your heart is now and has always been . . . when you're fulfilling a destiny that you know, without a doubt, is the reason you entered into a lifetime on this planet, you'll have easy access to

Source Energy, the Zone, the ether, the Nova, or whatever you want to call it. But you must make a conscious decision to tap into this place.

This is why many who individuals who want to be rock stars for the money and fame never make it. And many who *do* enjoy a period of success usually find it to be short-lived—their time onstage often destroyed by drugs, overspending, or not having enough energy to sustain long-term success. That's because their spirit never fully lined up with their false sense of destiny; their desire never fully aligned with creating music that would touch the hearts of others.

The same goes for you when thinking about having $10 million appear in your bank account. If you're not fully lined up, you'll likely associate this sudden loot with immediately quitting your miserable job. Your first inclination will be to get away from what you *don't* want. Then, after you've gotten tired of traveling the world, at some point, hopefully, you'll want to fully line up with your purpose. But why wait? Why don't you figure that out now?

Last year I was talking to a colleague who asked me to put myself in the same scenario: "If you had ten million in a bank account and you could do anything you wanted, what would it be?"

Without skipping a beat, I said, "I'd be a writer. All I'd do is write." He didn't skip a beat either. "Well, why don't you do that now? Even just do a little bit each day."

And that's how this book came to be born. I finally decided to take action *now* rather than wait for a perfect alignment of the stars or when I got a better handle on my business or when my daughter graduated high school (she's only eleven) or when I had more time or knew more . . . or when this or that happened. Finally, I made it happen.

You, too, can tap into the Universe and let it guide you in this process. Go in without judgments or preconceptions or negativity. Be willing to follow through with, and take action on, any and all plans that are given to you. Trust that your path will unfold as you begin your journey. Grab on to your destiny!

Just Know . . .

Your life is a work in progress. As far as your soul is concerned, it is infinite, with no beginning or end. For both body and soul, you will continue to evolve in so many ways that you can't even imagine. However, when you get into a high-vibratory feeling state, you can get a sneak peak into your evolution. No matter how uncertain you believe your life is right now, the moment you raise your energy, you'll feel an *inner knowing* that all is and always will be okay. Change is normal, but to remain stagnant is not, particularly where your soul is concerned.

Once you bring yourself into the Zone, your exhaustion, chaos, and worries will melt away. Even better, you'll be inspired to make the changes in your life that will excite you and put you into the *flow*. You'll be guided to only do the things that offer you the greatest results while enjoying a sense of well-being, peace, and happiness.

It may seem counterproductive to let go and go with the flow, especially if you want to take charge of your path. But once you understand that the Universe will only move in the direction in which your vibration is flowing, along with harnessing the core *knowing* of your purpose, you'll be at ease. Once you're confident that you're on the path to your destiny, your conscious/subconscious mind will plot to make your dreams a reality. With the power of the Universe conspiring to make it all happen, you will then become truly unstoppable.

Chapter Fourteen

THE THIRTEENTH STEP TOWARD RICHES: HOW TO USE THE POWER OF THE SIXTH SENSE

Your intuition knows what to do. The trick is getting your head to shut up so you can hear.

—LOUISE SMITH

When I was twenty-one, I hesitated while locking my apartment door as I was heading out. I had a feeling that I'd forgotten something. But as I stood there, I realized it was more than that; it was as if someone were calling out to me. It couldn't have been more than five seconds, and I couldn't figure it out, so I locked up, went out to my car, and drove away. But just as I got to the end of my block, a gold Mercedes-Benz blew through the light. If not for those five seconds where I'd paused at my door, I knew I would have been hit, perhaps even dying in the collision. I've since figured out that the someone "calling out to me" was the Universe telling me to really *listen*. A higher force was giving me an important message, and I will be eternally grateful for that. There have also been many other times when it protected me from danger.

I find that one of the benefits of having this connection to something greater is having the most vivid dreams just about every single night. They're like Hollywood movies—crystal clear, colorful, and many times seeming to have a complete storyline.

I realize that some of my dreams are messages from other planes of existence, with some of them being predictions about the future. Many times I get "teleported" to the Other Side to meet deceased people from all walks of life. Just as I'm honored to have this connection for some greater purpose, I've also benefited from it personally through fantastic gifts from this higher state of being.

One of those gifts is the realization that I can dream while I'm awake. And you can, too, by connecting with Source Energy and letting it send you messages about anything and everything—particularly answers to questions you may have about what to do next in your life or for help in making a monumental life decision. I'm talking about something Napoleon Hill described in *Think and Grow Rich* as the *sixth sense*:

> The SIXTH SENSE is that portion of the subconscious mind which has been referred to as the Creative Imagination. It has also been referred to as the "receiving set" through which ideas, plans, and thoughts flash into the mind. The "flashes" are sometimes called "hunches" or "inspirations."
>
> The sixth sense defies description! It cannot be described to a person who has not mastered the other principles of this philosophy, because such a person has no knowledge, and no experience with which the sixth sense comes only by meditation through mind development *from within*. The sixth sense probably is the medium of contact between the finite mind of man and Infinite Intelligence, and for this reason, *it is a mixture of both the mental and the spiritual*. It is believed to be the point at which the mind of math contacts the Universal Mind. . . .
>
> There is a power, or a First Clause, or an Intelligence, which permeates every atom of matter, and embraces every unit of energy perceptible to man—that this Infinite Intelligence covers acorns into oak trees, causes water to flow down hill in response to the law of gravity, follows night with day, and winter with summer, each maintaining its proper place and relationship to the other. This Intelligence may, through

the principles of this philosophy, be induced to aid in transmuting DESIRES into concrete, or material form. The author has this knowledge, because he has experimented with it—and has EXPERIENCED IT.

◈══◼══◈

Omens and Signs

My daughter recently decided that she wanted to go back to school after having been homeschooled for a short period of time. In general, I knew it was a good idea, but I was really nervous about it because in the past, her innocent little soul had been crushed by bullying. I settled myself down and reconnected with Source Energy, putting a feeling of trust out there, knowing I'd be guided in the right direction. Then I *let go*. One of the decisions I had to make was which of the two schools in our neighborhood would be a better fit for her. When I got to the first school, I felt a sense of dread in my gut. It was clear that one was a no-go.

When I got to the second school, an elderly crossing guard was in front shepherding the kids safely across the street. He cracked the biggest grin and gave me a thumbs-up as I drove by. I took that as a sign and enrolled her in the school that very day. Since starting there, my daughter has been so happy. She has amazing friends, an incredible teacher, and absolutely loves the curriculum. I don't remember ever seeing her as content with school as she is right now.

Omens, signs, and symbols are there for you, too, when you need guidance. They come in all different forms: crossing guards, dreams, serendipity, and so much more. As Napoleon Hill said in *Think and Grow Rich*:

> Somewhere in the cell-structure of the brain, is located an organ which receives vibrations of thought ordinarily called "hunches." So far, science has not discovered where this organ

of the sixth sense is located, but this is not important. The fact remains that human beings do receive accurate knowledge, through sources other than the physical senses. Such knowledge, generally, is received when the mind is under the influence of extraordinary stimulation. Any emergency which arouses the emotions, and causes the heart to beat more rapidly than normal may, and generally does, bring the sixth sense into action. Anyone who has experienced a near accident while driving, knows that on such occasions, the sixth sense often comes to one's rescue, and aids, by split seconds, in avoiding the accident.

<hr>

Your sixth sense comes from a direct connection between you and Source Energy. The cleaner your connection, the more tuned in you are. Some of what your sixth sense tells you will be whispered or discussed or even shouted out. Quiet your mind, raise your energy levels, and *listen*. Simply listen.

Chapter Fifteen

THE FOURTEENTH STEP TOWARD RICHES: MOVING BEYOND FEAR

Thinking will not overcome fear but action will.

—W. CLEMENT STONE

At the break of dawn on April 28, 1998, a dozen FBI agents kicked in the door of my home, swarmed around me, then rifled through every inch of my home seizing paperwork, computers, files, cash, and anything else they viewed as relevant to their investigation. All my financial assets were frozen. My car was seized, as was my mother's—both of which had been paid off in full. One thing they didn't seize was real estate—not that they wouldn't have liked to, but they didn't because they couldn't, as I didn't own any property free and clear. Although I had tons of equity, the bank still owned my home. About ten days later, probably the time it took for another search warrant, they raided my office. After that, there would be nothing left for the FBI to seize.

At the time, I only had a vague idea what was going on. For the next week or two, an FBI agent called and said he wanted to sit down with me to talk, but he wouldn't tell me about what. He simply refused to tell me why my assets had been seized.

I was only twenty years old at the time. I had a small home-based business, and I didn't yet know about the legal and financial responsibilities involved in starting and running one. I also didn't know enough about love. I'd married far too young—to a foreigner who was seven years older than I was and eons beyond my understanding of the darker side of human beings. I married for love; he married for a green card. He beat me up physically on a regular basis, but even worse was the mental and emotional abuse. He was also a cocaine addict, selling drugs to support his habit, and keeping women on the side to support his other habit.

My little home-based business was about the only thing that gave me a spark during that time. It made me feel as if I had some control over my life. I thought I was doing well enough financially and that I had things figured out—that is, until my business started to fall apart. It went from being the daylight I needed for financial freedom to escape an abusive marriage to becoming a cataclysmic abyss of financial ruin and legal disaster.

Six months later, on October 26, 1998, eight FBI agents, four deputies, and four Orange County sheriffs swooped in and arrested me while I was visiting my mother in San Clemente, California. I was charged with a myriad of federal crimes. And after a year and a half in federal detention centers as a pretrial defendant unable to raise bail, I finally took a four-year prison deal to find my way out of this nightmare.

Having a lot of time to think was my way out. Initially I felt like a victim, and in some sense I was, but I ultimately realized that everything that happened was *my responsibility* on so many different levels. I vowed to do better. Much better.

After being released from prison, I quickly discovered that getting a decent-paying job with a felony on my record was nearly impossible. So, instead, I decided to build a multimillion-dollar enterprise on my own from scratch. The next phase of my life introduced me to commodity trading. I not only enjoyed trading, but I was also extremely good at it. Since I also enjoyed (and still do) sharing my success, I decided to offer a forecasting newsletter on futures trading in addition to conducting a handful of related seminars.

I wish I could say that I put my past behind me back then, but I can't. It would take me many more years to realize that I still held on to this "ghost"—anger at the deepest levels imaginable over the injustice seemingly inflicted upon me—on a deep vibrational level. As a result, I was subconsciously vibrating with anger, and what do you know? I attracted a battle with the Commodity Futures Trading Commission (CFTC) that sparked an investigation into my company. Shortly thereafter, they froze my assets and filed a civil lawsuit against me and several of my companies.

My attorneys argued for my First Amendment right of free speech; the CFTC argued that I was in violation of their regulations. They kept on pounding a square peg into a round hole, struggling to make a case that my newsletter had put me into the category of being an adviser and therefore was subject to their regulations. (A new law has since been passed affirming a publisher's First Amendment rights, including newsletter publishers like me.)

I fought this battle for two years. What cost the most was my diminishing strength, my lack of belief in myself, and my inability to create new things. I knew that the faster I cut bait, the faster I could get on a new path of creation and positivity, so I settled the case, went back to keeping my vibes flying high, and started attracting only what was at the top of the pyramid.

By letting go of my past, including all the harsh judgments others had about me and those I had about myself, I was able to *surrender to a state of complete forgiveness* . . . and was free. Through the power of raising my vibrations consistently and consciously, Source Energy was able to heal what I'd been carrying on my back for a lifetime.

The Zone can heal *anything* in your life, from a broken heart to a disease, including things that you're not even aware are "off" in some way. So raise your energy vibrations and bask in the power of Source Energy. Allow it to heal you in the ways you most need healing.

Shedding the Ghosts of the Past with Love and Forgiveness

The events that you've experienced in your past can cause a vibrational *lingering* that runs as bloatware in the back of your subconscious mind. They can cause vibratory feelings of failure, loss, cynicism, distrust, victimhood, anger, resentment, depression, hopelessness, or just plain old fear.

It took many difficult years for me to get to a pure feeling state of loving those who I viewed as having caused me so much injustice—in particular, the government prosecutors. But I got to a good place by doing the following:

1. Understanding that those who worked on my cases thought they were being ethical in their investigations. Based on my business activities at that time, I can definitely see that their reasoning was justified.
2. Appreciating all that the government does for us, including being responsible for the streets we drive on, the water we drink, the national parks we treasure, and the defense of democracy.
3. Sending out feelings of love, understanding, and compassion to those involved in my cases—especially extending forgiveness to those who I felt operated with vindictiveness.

But mostly, I had to forgive myself. I had *become* the negative labels others pinned on me—guilty, depressed, and unfortunate—until I realized that I could give myself my own labels—responsible, grateful, and resilient. Like a snake shedding its skin, with each passing day, you, too, can shed your old you and become wiser. You are a soul in constant flux.

Just Say "Forget It!" and Let It Go

You are the only one standing in your own way. The faster you come to terms with this reality, the faster you can break free of the obstacles you've created.

The first hurdle I let go of was my ordeal from two decades ago: I was barely old enough to make adult decisions for myself but also unaware of the consequences of my decisions, the most painful one being unwittingly exposed to legal jeopardy as a result of the actions of my ex-husband. Finally, I said to myself, "Let it go! Learn, forgive, and move forward in a positive and empowering direction."

My second obstacle to let go of was my almost nonexistent sense of self-worth. My low self-esteem, overreactions to criticism, obsessions with the past, and more, dominated me in the form of indecision, doubt, and fear! I worked on raising my energy to get into the Zone. One of the most awesome things about that state is that indecision, doubt, and fear cannot exist there. Finally, I was able to accept myself for the perfect soul that I am today, always have been, and always will be.

Napoleon Hill, in *Think and Grow Rich*, wrote about his own understanding of this dynamic:

> INDECISION is the seedling of FEAR! Remember this, as you read. Indecision crystallizes into DOUBT, the two blend and become FEAR! The "blending" process often is slow. This is one reason why these three enemies are so dangerous. They germinate and grow *without their presence being observed.*
>
> *Fears are nothing more than states of mind.* One's state of mind is subject to control and direction. Physicians, as everyone knows, are less subject to attack by disease than ordinary laymen, for the reason that physicians DO NOT FEAR DISEASE. Physicians, without fear or hesitation, have been known to physically contact hundreds of people, daily, who were suffering from such contagious diseases such as smallpox, without becoming infected. Their immunity against the disease consisted, largely, if not solely, in their absolute lack of FEAR.
>
> Man can create nothing which he does not first conceive in the form of an impulse of thought. Following the statement, comes another still greater importance, namely, MAN's THOUGHT IMPULSES BEGIN IMMEDIATELY TO TRANSLATE THEMSELVES INTO THEIR PHYSICAL EQUIVALENT,

WHETHER THOSE THOUGHTS ARE VOLUNTARY OR INVOL-UNTARY. Thought impulses which are picked up through the ether, by mere chance (thoughts which have been released by other minds) may determine one's financial, business, professional, or social destiny just as surely as do the thought impulses which one creates by intent and design.

Preface to the Lost Chapters

....

The Universe is God.
I am God so that means I am the Universe.

—OSCAR WILDE

....

People all around you are constantly dishing out shallow, irrelevant, and confusing information, leading you to feel disconnected, unsure about yourself and the world around you, and forgetful that you always have an inner guidance system that will *never* give you erroneous directions.

However, you can't just rely on magic to get you back on track. In the same way that thinking positive thoughts is a fruitless exercise without acting upon them, so, too, is receiving guidance without taking action. For example, I found that my life began to change in leaps and bounds when I deleted Facebook from my phone and stopped watching the nightly news. I swapped getting angry over politics for dusting off old dreams I'd abandoned. Now that I realize that *everything* is possible, I soak in all I can each and every day, and intend to continue to do so until it's my time to exit from this physical plane.

This brings us to the opportunity to soak in something truly remarkable. What follows is what I believe to be the Lost Chapters of Napoleon Hill's *Think and Grow Rich*. I can see why they would have been cut from the book when it was first published in 1937, as it was a time when television wasn't a *thing*—people didn't binge-watch or veg out in front of the tube for hours and hours every day (the latest findings show that today, the average US adult watches more than five hours of TV on a daily basis). And even though radio was a big deal then, most people had a life involving family, work, and play. Listening to the radio was not the primary activity filling their time.

The 1930s was also very tumultuous for America and the entire world. There was a widespread negative outlook about the future, mostly due to the aftermath of the Depression and signs of what would soon become the unspeakable crimes against humanity perpetrated during World War II. It was easy for charlatans to prey on those in need of hope by selling them on get-rich-quick schemes. They "sold" positive attitudes, thinking, and feelings without having the integrity to inform people that it took much more than that, and thus their messages became synonymous with worthless tonics being hawked by snake-oil salesmen.

That is the backdrop against which *Think and Grow Rich* was released. In the two Lost Chapters, Napoleon Hill recommended closing off negative talkers and thinkers, including family and friends. In fact, he believed that to progress to heights of success and wealth, it is a requirement to do so. It's interesting that he said this at a time (during the Great Depression) when doing anything like it was very unpopular, if not absolutely impractical. Few people could afford to ditch family and friends. People needed one another—in fact, that's all they had.

I believe that Napoleon Hill, if he were alive today, would also require cutting out negative media, *including* social media. He'd require that everyone completely "unplug" from brain-rotting and spirit-robbing vices *and* devices. What most don't realize is that a major reason why they feel out of control and desolate is because they let in corrupt thoughts that alter their perceptions, feelings, and overall faith in life itself.

So choose to disconnect from these energy drainers, and *reconnect* with the Source of all energy. Understand the power it offers. In the same way that Napoleon Hill wrote about alchemists and wizards of the past who turned lead into gold, do the same to manifest your own burning desire.

TRANSCENDING ABOVE THE COMMON MAN

As you begin to ascend the ladder of success and abundance, critics will come from all corners to make you doubt your plan and question your abilities to reach your goal of accumulating money. You will find that it will take continuous determination, poise, and persistence as you slowly make progress toward greater achievement.

In previous chapters, you were instructed to take organized steps in translating your BURNING DESIRES into its monetary equivalent in the form of a DEFINITE practical plan, or set of plans, through which this abundance could be attained. With repeated instructions to the subconscious mind through repeated AUTO-SUGGESTION, you will begin to convince the subconscious mind that you shall have what you fix your mind to achieve.

But ahead lies a great danger for any man who dares to step beyond the opinions and influences of a middling society. Those around you of lowly thinking will grapple to permanently handicap your conscious thinking toward the promise of abundance and prosperity. It then becomes an arduous task of carrying out the thirteen principles while exhausting energy to ward off the tawdry cackling of negativity and constant criticism of your goals.

The fact that most every person of whom you associate is seeking an opportunity to acquire money should not give you safe ground to openly reveal ANY plans to accumulate money. Inferior minds will take great delight in your defeat, because they envy you and your plans to become successful.

As a reminder to yourself to follow this advice, put into action your goal ahead of you while keeping a closed mouth about your plans. Then tell the world what you intend to do only by showing it. It is through your actions, not words, that count the most.

Despite your best efforts to conceal your plans and actions toward higher achievement, just the mere act of moving toward something greater around those who believe in lack and failure can hinder your ability to reach your goals of wealth.

"Birds of a feather flock together," they say. You will find early on in your transition from lack to abundance that it will become necessary to retreat from those of negative thoughts and opinions, particularly when referring to your plan, or plans, when marching on to the heights of financial status.

This cross-roads in the path of every man and woman on the threshold of prosperity will determine, more than anything else, whether the DEFINITE GOAL will be reached. People of lower thinking and negative beliefs will destroy victory in reaching a chosen goal. You will be forced to make a difficult choice between riches and poverty if you decide against removing those who do not support your highest vision and conscious thought behavior. This is, perhaps, the most painful decision you must make when beginning to reach your goals of prosperity.

But how does one overcome a low vibration person or environment if suddenly held hostage by such? Immediate removal of lowly vibration offenders filled with negative thoughts becomes necessary if one truly desires to transcend into higher vibratory states of being. If one is found trapped in a low vibration environment, finding an outlet to freedom from circumstances such as these is wholly necessary to transcend into higher vibration altitudes.

To exist among men who are similar in the ways they think, feel, and act can only encourage you to become the same. To rid yourself of people you have always known can be difficult. But it becomes *required* otherwise your DETERMINA-TION, DEFINITENESS OF PURPOSE, the DESIRE TO ATTAIN

THE GOAL, AUTO-SUGGESTION and the PERSISTENT EFFORT needed to accumulate money will all be in vain!

You will find yourself in the awkward position of having to decide to discontinue social calls to those who do not emulate the same like mind, as the one you have acquired upon using the principles I have illustrated in this book. It may make you question some of the wisdom of the principles I have taught you, or make you doubt your plan to accumulate money. Have Faith in yourself; have Faith in the Infinite. These feelings of doubt are normal. And as you move forward into your DEFINITE OF PURPOSE mixed with FAITH, you will find positive friends and acquaintances on the other side awaiting you!

People of negative thinking have a subconscious desire to see all of those around them to experience the same walk of life. They will do whatever they can to cling to limiting beliefs and negative thinking because a life of which they are familiar is more comfortable than facing a change of stupendous proportions. Perhaps they believe the criticism of your plan to accumulate money is well meaning advice. Despite this fact, you must distance yourself from all criticism and negativity if you are to experience abundance and prosperity.

You will find that once you permanently disassociate from those who are averse to the person of wealth of whom you desire to become, you will feel empowered and free from the grips of negativity that were previously binding you, causing a hindrance to the attainment of your BURNING DESIRE.

At the very beginning of this book, I included the story of Edwin C. Barnes and how he made the trip to Orange, N.J. by freight train to meet Thomas A. Edison. Barnes had a DOMINATING DESIRE to partner with Edison no matter what it would take. By Barnes leaving behind his old circumstances, acquaintances, and friends behind to become part of a new environment, he was quickly able to change his thinking by submerging himself with new thoughts and among positive acquaintances. To do this, he had to remove himself from his known environment to seek out an unknown environment to achieve his DEEPEST BURNING DESIRE to eventually become a business partner with Mr. Edison!

For a man to leave behind his settled life to go to a large extent to fulfill a DOMINATING DESIRE to make it a physical reality, despite the stakes at hand, is quite remarkable! Barnes was probably unaware at that time but for him to completely remove himself from the life he knew well to set out for a new life was the requisite to achieve his greatest vision.

You may not have the same willingness as Barnes, to leave the life you know to enter into a new world that is unknown to you. It takes great courage to make this kind of change to bring about a new destiny. But note well, this kind of radical change may not be altogether necessary for most to achieve their burning desires.

Every person needs a change of mental and physical environment at regular intervals, the same as a change and variety of food and clothing are necessary. This keeps your mind alert and in a state to receive a storm of new ideas, outside of one's own daily environment.

The idea factory inside of your mind becomes more awake and receptive to new vibrations, that of which a new environment can offer. When these new ideas appear, they will usually rush into your mind in the form of sudden "inspirations." These thoughts of inspiration are usually direct messages from Infinite Intelligence and is of the utmost importance, which means you *must* act upon them as soon as you receive these thoughts. Failure to do so is equivalent to rejecting the Divine Plan for which Infinite Intelligence has formed the best path of stepping stones to your BURNING DESIRE.

By rejecting the inspiration from Infinite Intelligence will put the achievement of your goal in jeopardy, because likely these 'flashes' of inspirational thoughts and ideas will cease to appear in the future instances since you will have shown Infinite Intelligence that you have no use for the ideas you have received. This idea factory that is connected to Infinite Intelligence does not die, though it may become dormant through lack of use. This is why it becomes necessary to follow these messages of inspiration as they are received as to continuously receive more direction from Infinite Intelligence.

Be cognizant of the negativity that surrounds you in your daily environment and be willing to eliminate those who talk of poverty and illness. Be willing to dismiss those of negative and destructive natures at the drop of a hat. If you fail to quickly seize thoughts, ideas, words, and actions of doubt, poverty, indecision, or disbelief—regardless of the origin—you will find yourself hopelessly doomed to mediocrity and poverty.

But how do you know if an acquaintance or member of your family is of a low vibration of negativity and dark thoughts? Try this as an experiment: when around the person you are uncertain of, speak only in positive tones. Only communicate positive subject matter around this person.

One who is off-put by your positive talk will eventually form a critical opinion of the conversation. He may attempt to change the subject to something negative, or he may abruptly dismiss himself from your presence. This is how you can be certain that an acquaintance is pulsating a low vibration level of thought. To socialize with negative thinking people will not serve you and your pursuits of reaching a chosen goal.

It can be a devastating task to take the necessary action in removing those who do not serve a higher good but it becomes a requirement for those who are consciously choosing riches over poverty. To allow those who rally for a life of lack and poverty to participate in your daily environment will bring to you dire consequences indeed. It will take great courage to distance yourself from those who do not serve a greater benefit, but it is necessary in your rise to altitudes of achievement.

This is well thought in a poem written by Rudyard Kipling:

If
If you can keep your head when all about you
Are losing theirs and blaming it on you;
If you can trust yourself when all men doubt you,
But make allowance for their doubting too:
If you can wait and not be tired by waiting,
Or, being lied about, don't deal in lies,
Or being hated don't give way to hating,
And yet don't look too good, nor talk too wise;

If you can dream—and not make dreams your master;
If you can think—and not make thoughts your aim,

If you can meet with Triumph and Disaster
And treat those two impostors just the same:
If you can bear to hear the truth you've spoken
Twisted by knaves to make a trap for fools,
Or watch the things you gave your life to, broken,
And stoop to build 'em with worn-out tools;

Of you can make one heap of all your winnings
And risk it on one turn of pitch-and-toss,
And lose, and start again at your beginnings,
And never breathe a word about your loss:
If you can force your heart and nerve and sinew
To serve your turn long after they are gone,
And so hold on when there is nothing in you
Except the Will which says to them: "Hold on!"

If you can talk with crowds and keep your virtue,
Or walk with Kings—nor lose the common touch,
If neither foes nor loving friends can hurt you,
If all men count with you, but none too much:
If you can fill the unforgiving minute
Within sixty seconds' worth of distance run,
Yours is the Earth and everything that's in it,
And—which is more—you'll be a Man, my son!

Man and the ways of the world will always be amiss, firing its destructive impulses in your direction. What has gone "wrong" with our fellow man in their thinking, belief systems and lack of ambition? In many instances, you may find it easy to succumb to their limited ways of living if you're not careful. Be warned! Thinking, believing, behaving, and feeling as the common man and woman will limit you in every way as long as you choose to sink to their lowly station in life.

How does one transcend above this powerful mass state of mind of most who are living today? This is the "deceit" you must practice with mind. And it is the "deceit" of raising your vibrations with a clear conscious state of mind that must never falter but for a single moment, maintaining the state of mind known as a BURNING DESIRE TO WIN which is essential to success.

This will be the challenge you will be forced to maintain both day and night. It will be a fight, a battle for which must be won! To lose would mean certain death—that of your mind and spirit—the two factors required to reach the heights of achievement at which you are aiming. To do this, you must constantly work to surpass the limitations of the common man. This will take constant effort of which you must be willing to endure and prevail.

Many men strain to destroy one another, mostly due to doubt in one's self. You must learn to embrace higher vibrations while ignoring the negativity that constantly toils about, of which it is the obstacle to ensure that you never succeed in the goals you desire. Reminders of negativity, doubt, poverty, and failure are all around you and it does not take but a brief moment to find it. It will take a strong sense of inner will to overcome these low vibrations that will unceasingly take hold of your ankles to keep pulling you down to its lowly level.

This is the reason why most who are born into impoverished conditions never rise above their circumstances. It is because they have come to accept their surroundings as their "misfortune" and something they cannot overcome. Because of this fact, many will hardly try, as they have come to accept their indigent circumstances as their permanent environment. To rise above this long enough with the energy required to accumulate money is nearly impossible for someone who sees nothing but poverty around him. To convince the mind that there are riches abound when all one sees is lack is almost impossible to overcome without APPLIED PERSISTENCE and a BURNING DESIRE for greater achievement.

What can we do when having been born into such impoverished circumstances? This is where the 'deceit' comes. It calls for the 'deceit' of the mind to such a degree that one believes in endless possibilities and prosperity for themselves no matter what they may see around them as their environment.

Perhaps this is the most difficult part in all of this, to actively deceive the mind to believe in riches when one looks around only to see poverty is a seemingly insurmountable task. Take heed! *For nothing is impossible!* Not only is it possible to transcend above negative beliefs, but once you understand how to alter your pulsating vibration to higher levels, you will surely see a new abundant life unfold before your very eyes, *faster than you ever thought possible!*

To do this, you must have FAITH in reaching into a world of the unseen or the ether. Infinite Intelligence is in all things living. It is within this energy that permeates through all things that you must place an unwavering BELIEF in. This is a most difficult undertaking: to "deceive" the mind into believing what is not while surrounded by the unfortunate of circumstances in an environment made up of mostly doom-sayers and ne'er-do-wells. But it can be done with continuous FAITH and action toward a DEFINITE PLAN.

The depression made many men falter, bringing most to their knees. But if you are so inclined as to look closer, you will discover that a wealthy man whose riches were but extinguished by the depression had either already began to regain his wealth or found himself well on his way in a short time. This is because wealth is <u>within</u> him. It is not something he must reach outside of himself to access. He already has the BELIEF in the attainment of wealth in his mind. With FAITH and a DEFINITE PLAN to regain his financial status, it becomes only a short time before he is able to claim his wealth once again.

However, money in the hands of one who did not acquire it gradually, is often fatal to success. Quick riches are more dangerous than poverty because it does not allow for the mind to adjust to a sudden windfall of money. If the mind is used to poverty, receiving large sums of money quickly confuses the mind that hasn't yet developed the self-worth and skills needed to keep and grow the money received. It is then quickly lost just as fast as it was received!

How to "Tune In" to Wealth

To best accurately describe this is by using my radio channel example. A wealthy man who has had a direct connection to the unseen world of abundance will never have to worry about a life of poverty regardless of what his temporary circumstances has brought him.

Contrary, a poor man who has unintentionally stumbled upon riches will find himself in the poor house once more because he is only tuned in to the beliefs, vibrations, and mind of poverty and lack.

For many, it can be difficult to comprehend how one can believe and 'feel' prosperous when circumstances everywhere show quite a different reality. In all fairness, it can seem like a problematic undertaking to 'feel' wealthy when you have bought into the belief that you are poor and always will be. How can one possibly feel rich when poverty is all around? How can one believe that riches are afoot when men are standing in soup lines as far as the eye can see?

You must pay particular attention to the fact that not everyone is impoverished. Perhaps venturing out to an opulent part of town is your first order of business. Make the effort to notice and observe those who are prosperous. There are many! Particularly still, during the times of depression there are those who remained very wealthy. Some gained more wealth faster than ever before while, at the same time, most were experiencing extreme financial hardship. You can decide to ignore poverty; choose instead to open your eyes and see the abundance and opportunity all around you all of the time. This is where the inner toggling of the mind begins when you can choose to "tune out" poverty and "tune in" prosperity. This is a very simple and subtle change in what you *choose* to observe and focus on, beginning with "tuning in" to a different channel.

Somewhere in your cellular make-up lies the seed of desire that, once aroused and put into CONSTANT ACTION while "tuning in" to wealth, can carry you to great heights of achievement and success. With a BURNING DESIRE comes a plan, or plans, for attainment, many times hidden in the whispers of the ethers. With plans comes taking actionable steps toward achievement. With action comes the faith to eliminate all doubt and negative thinking. Then comes persistence because with unrelenting persistence will bring success.

Any unyielding BURNING DESIRE, of which all other success principles are applied, will bring forth your desires. These principles, when applied continuously, NEVER FAIL!

Remember, you are the master of your own mind, which has the power to alter the course of your destiny, and you must practice the daily discipline to carefully scrutinize and control your thoughts. You will find that if you believe you cannot, you will not. But if you believe you can do it, you will.

SUMMONING DESIRES THROUGH THE ETHER

On this morning, I had awoke to the thought that all things are made of the finest of particles, those that are unseen and intangible. And it is within these finite particles of which all things are created, especially those that are hidden to the human eye.

I decided to explore the depths of these fine particles to further explain the connection between these and our thoughts. I find it odd how no scientist has yet been able to explain the connection between these fine particles and our thoughts. It would seem that science has only managed to build theories of logic to support their limited understanding of how the unseen works.

But I thought to myself, "How does one explain the unseen? There is so much that is unknown! How can the limited human brain possibly prove the power of positive thinking and the manifestation of a BURNING DESIRE, beginning from nothing more than a feeling at the base of my gut? How limited we are to attempt a haphazard theory of such a powerful force! And do we have to completely understand the bridge between our thoughts and the seen and unseen particles that surround us to understand how to use this powerful force to summon wealth?"

These and many other questions grew within me as I remembered reading a paper many years ago that illustrated a drawing of an atom and how there is a magnetic force field of sorts of which multiple atoms are attracted, or "magnetized" together to make a molecule. When many molecules

179

are attracted to one another, they eventually make the solid things we see when we look around. What was most significant about this illustration was that there seemed to be nothing in between the finest of these finite particles!

Certainly science has found a theory to explain how these finite particles can exist in our world but what they have *failed* to explain is how they are magnetized in such a way to create the particle (an atom) in the first place when the space between is made up of nothingness! This could only mean, perhaps, that the attraction of such particles within the void of nothingness of which it exists, *just is*. I am interested to know how science plans to explain this in the form of theory or hypothesis one day.

For now it would seem that our understanding of these fine particles and how they have come to exist from nothing remains a mystery, because it is something that cannot be explained in text or by complex illustration.

By my observation, it would seem that these fine particles exist by only the 'thought' of its source or Infinite Intelligence. If it is the 'thought' of Infinite Intelligence that magnetizes the smallest of particles together from a void of nothing, then we can assume to have the same ability to use our thoughts to "think" fine particles together to form the "thing" of our desires. To do this would require an unwavering FAITH of which not a single doubt can exist to "think" these fine particles into any configuration of our liking.

Infinite Intelligence does not hold doubt or fear in its ability to create all that we see and do not see from a void of nothing. All that you see, from the flowers and the trees to more dense things like automobiles and freight trains, are all created by Infinite Intelligence from nothing . . . *beginning from a thought*! If Infinite Intelligence has this remarkable power, *so do you!*

The difference between Infinite Intelligence and the common man or woman is its emotional "feeling," or *knowing*, that what it "thinks" into reality, so shall it be. This author, being neither a scientist nor a man of the cloth, is inclined to believe that every man and woman holds this same power within because we are all a part of this same source power. We are all part of this Infinite Intelligence and always will be. Of course, we hold this power of creation because we were created by Infinite Intelligence from the beginning of time!

The time will come when schools will teach the "science of creation." It is then that this knowledge of creation will be accepted as a science. When that time comes, no man, woman, or child will approach Infinite Intelligence in a state of doubt or fear, for the reason that there will be no such emotion as doubt or fear. I fancy the day when this occurs, but it is unlikely that it will happen in my lifetime.

Why do so many choose lack over abundance? Why do most refuse to use this source power that has always been available to all of us since birth? It is because we have ceased in our belief and knowledge of the existence of such power. Many have long forgotten how to use these powers that are, and always have been, available in an instant, by simply calling upon it.

There is a reason that the alchemists of the centuries past have had the ability to turn lead into gold and water into wine. Do you believe this was a fallacy, only to exist in children's story books and tales of folklore?

Contrary to this belief, there were ancient alchemists who knew of the power of the source in changing the vibration of the fine particles within any given object to transmute it into something different by pulsating a powerful force of vibration through the ether.

Imagine an alchemist who possessed the power to transform a brick of lead to that of the purest gold. He did this with the FAITH and BELIEF in the unseen while altering the waves of vibration through his thoughts, feelings, and emotions as he would emit this unbridled power through the ether to COMMAND this transformation at once! This "magic," as such, was commonplace during periods of human history. This "magic" seems to have been lost over the centuries.

Insofar I believe this power was purposely hidden from the public by the kings of the time to never allow the common man to possess these powerful attributes. Since then, these legacies have since been reduced to myths and stories of folklore with the idea of having man forget about the existence of such remarkable power.

Their plan to eliminate these secrets from history proved to be successful. Most have forgotten that these powers exist in all men and women from birth and is a necessity along with the ingredients of BURNING DESIRE and FAITH to bring about anything of the mind's desire into reality! This POWER is *essential* for the accumulation of wealth and to rise to the heights of greater achievement.

Children have an innate desire to believe in all things magical. They will use play to act out a show of magic with staged parlor tricks and concocted magical potions. But as children mature, the magic is stripped away as they are sold the idea that their magical world was nothing more than make-believe. Soon after, they recess into the doldrums of the public at large, leaving behind the magic they once thought of as being real.

This also applies to children who have reported having outer world experiences including that of seeing spirits that, upon telling an adult of these sightings, are admonished and condemned for 'imagining' things. They are further convinced that these experiences are not real and are nothing more than ideas from their imagination. How valuable it would be to possess this BELIEF and FAITH in magic throughout an entire lifetime!

The Application of Using Intangible Vibratory Forces

To apply intensely focused thought to a BURNING DESIRE is only part of what is required to translate a goal into reality. The most important detail of your application is to maintain a <u>constant</u> high level of vibration for the purpose of imbuing the finest of particles in the world of the unseen (ether) to bring to creation the coveted goal.

It is important that you understand that positive and negative vibrations cannot occupy the mind and body at the same time. Lower vibration feelings cannot exist while higher vibration feelings abound! Lower vibratory feelings are the seedlings of poverty and can only bring to you much of the same if you fail to remove these emotions as much as possible. Whether pulsating from people or situations, to express a lower vibratory 'feeling' and emotion is to attract a similar vibration in the form of 'bad luck,' or unfortunate circumstances.

Any high vibratory impulse of thought and 'feeling' which is repeatedly pulsated by force through the ether will be, finally, accepted and mutually met by Infinite Intelligence, which proceeds to translate that impulse of vibratory 'feeling' into its physical equivalent.

Consider again the statement, ALL THOUGHTS WHICH HAVE BEEN EMOTIONALIZED (given the 'feeling' of BURNING DESIRE), WITH A HIGHER VIBRATION AND MIXED WITH FAITH WILL BEGIN IMMEDIATELY TO TRANSLATE THEMSELVES INTO THEIR PHYSICAL EQUIVALENT. What is 'magnetized' to you is following the vibration of which you are vibrating through the ether.

The emotions, or the "feeling" portion of thoughts is the act of pulsating a vibration through the ether, and it is within these powerful vibrations that bring back its equivalent counterpart. The higher vibration will bring back its vibration equivalent, whether the impulse thought and "feeling" is for love, money, or achievement of some kind. The vibration which is pulsated into the ether is the equivalent of what will be mirrored and returned to you.

It becomes of greater importance, above all else, to closely scrutinize the "feelings" of emotion and the vibration of which are being pulsated into the ether, because Infinite Intelligence can only return what was originally given in the form of your vibrations.

There are millions of people who "feel" themselves doomed to lack and failure, because of some strange force over which they "feel" and BELIEVE they have no control. They are the creators of their own state of poverty, because of their negative "feelings" (vibrations) which are then received by the ether and translated into its perfect physical equivalent.

Your "feelings" of impulse or vibrations of your BURN-
ING DESIRE mixed with FAITH will translate into its physical, or monetary equivalent, particularly if waiting in a state
of expectancy or BELIEF that the transmutation will actually
take place. Your BELIEF, or FAITH, is the element which determines the actions of your subconscious mind. Your 'feelings'
of vibration is the necessary ingredient for prompting Infinite
Intelligence to respond with its vibration equivalent to bring
to you the same physical counterpart.

"Feelings" of having money will bring money. For someone who doesn't have money, there is nothing to hinder you
from "deceiving" your subconscious mind by having the
"feeling" that money is, indeed, coming.

This is, perhaps, the most difficult discipline in the practice of achieving wealth. You may ask, "How might I 'feel' as
though I have money when all I see is poverty around me?"

Remember, you must learn to "deceive" the subconscious
mind by "feeling" the vibration of money while having FAITH,
or BELIEF that the money will come very soon. THOUGHTS
WHICH ARE MIXED WITH ANY OF THE "FEELINGS" OF
EMOTIONS, CONSTITUTE A "MAGNETIC" FORCE WHICH
ATTRACTS, FROM THE VIBRATIONS OF THE ETHER, OTHER
SIMILAR PHYSICAL, OR MONETARY EQUIVALENTS. A vibration thus "magnetized" with the "feeling" of a high vibration
emotion will always attract its precise equivalent, or duplicate
counterpart.

If you look around and all you have experienced is poverty and failure, this is what has been "magnetized" to you
from the vibration equivalent of which you have pulsated
through the ether. Just as you have "magnetized" poverty,
instead you can change the "feelings" of vibration you are
pulsating to the ether to that of money and success. You have
the power to change the course of your reality by changing
the vibratory "feelings" you are sending into the ether.

In the beginning, I mentioned the success of Kate Smith,
and how for years she sang, without money, and without
price. What I didn't disclose was how she used her voice to
raise her vibration to beckon success to her through the "feelings" she pulsated through the ether as she sung in her daily

vocal practice. She used her voice to raise her vibration and used this high state of being to then 'call' success to her with the "feeling": that she had already made it on Broadway.

While countless singers had come and gone, they failed because they did not know how to pulsate the "feeling" that they were destined to be on Broadway. But not Miss Smith. She was able to conquer Broadway by transferring her BURN-ING DESIRE into thought and "feeling" vibrations that she pulsated through the ether with the BELIEF that she had already made it. And make it she did!

Broadway soon came calling, and when it did, Miss Smith named her price in figures so high that her one week's salary was more than what most people make in a year. And she did it by raising her vibrations to pulsate that 'feeling' of success during her daily vocal practice.

You can use the emotions of DESIRE, FAITH, LOVE, SEX, ENTHUSIASM, ROMANCE, HOPE, or any emotion of high vibration that can open a connection between you and Infinite Intelligence so that you may benefit from all of the greatness that this UNSEEN POWER has to offer. However, the negative emotions of FEAR, JEALOUSY, HATRED, REVENGE, GREED, SUPERSTITION and ANGER should be avoided because these emotions cannot bring to you any BURNING DESIRE of a higher vibration.

The power of FAITH and BELIEF mixed with emotional "feelings" and THOUGHT is the highest form of vibration known. This living, pulsating, vibratory energy which per-meates every atom of matter, and fills every niche of space, connects every human to Infinite Intelligence, or the source.

This Infinite Intelligence will, through the thirteen prin-ciples, be able to assist in transmuting DESIRES into con-crete, or material form, provided that one "magnetizes" these DESIRES through the practice of raising vibratory energy fre-quently and often. This is the Master Key to truly attracting the riches you desire.

This much the author does know: there is a power, or a source, or an Infinite Intelligence, which permeates *every* atom of matter, and embraces every unit of energy percepti-ble and concealed to man, and that this Infinite Intelligence is alive and well in *all* things. Without this Intelligence, *all matter would cease to exist*. The author has this knowledge, particularly that of using this Intelligence, because he used the connection to this power to bring these very words and success principles to you.

The space between the finite particles is very much alive, that it is the highest form of vibration known, excepting, perhaps, the vibration of THOUGHT which controls this "nothingness." You can choose to control this power to develop the life circumstances which you have always desired, or you can choose to be a victim of the lowly thoughts and vibrations you are releasing into the ethers. The possibility of the latter seems terrible, particularly because there is a choice, and bargaining for a life of poverty, instead of a life of enjoying abundance, is foolish.

Now that you know the practicability of the thirteen principles, it is time to apply this philosophy to accumulate riches through the transmutation of your desires. Do not delay a moment longer, for a world of great abundance awaits!

In parting, I would remind you that "life is a checkerboard, and the player opposite you is TIME. If you hesitate before moving, or neglect to move promptly, your men will be wiped off the board by TIME. You are playing against a partner who will not tolerate INDECISION!"

Previously you may have had a logical excuse for not having forced Life to come through with whatever you asked, but that alibi is now obsolete, because you are in possession of the Master Key that unlocks the door to Life's bountiful riches.

The Master Key is intangible, but it is powerful! It is the privilege of creating, in your own mind, a BURNING DESIRE for a definite form of riches. There is no penalty for the use of the Key, but there is a price you must pay if you do not use it. The price is FAILURE. There is a reward of stupendous proportions if you put the Key to use. It is the satisfaction that comes to all who conquer self and force life to pay whatever is asked.

The reward is worthy of your effort. Will you make the start and be convinced?

"If we were related," said the immortal Emerson, "we shall meet." In closing, may I borrow his thought, and say, "If we are related, we have, through these pages, met."

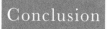

What I believe to be the two Lost Chapters *reveal* the *exact application* of vibratory forces for transforming your *burning desire into reality*! I've designed a powerful program to help bring Napoleon Hill's wisdom to you using the common language of today in an easy-to-follow step-by-step thirty-day plan. Only recently have I even begun sharing this plan publicly:

My 30-Day Success Plan

The Single Goal I Want to Achieve in the Next 30 Days Is:

_____

And the Way I'm Going to Do It Is by Accomplishing
These Critical Things Each Week:

Week 1

Week 2

Week 3

Week 4

First, start at the very top of the chart and write down your immediate goal that you believe you can accomplish in thirty days, which is likely to be part of a much larger burning desire.

Next, skip down to the Week 4 box. Do so to include any final step(s) and to manifest the attainment of your goal. In most cases, there are many things that occur each week that you've listed.

Now, go back up to the Week 1 box and begin working your way down through each week's box by using essentially the same brainstorming exercise we discussed earlier—just let a stream of ideas that you can do right away flow out, and jot them down as fast as they come in. In a flash, all four boxes will be filled up. You may need to do a little refining, but then be ready to start taking action on the ideas you wrote down for Week 1.

One of the indicators of whether your goal is a good fit for you is the ease or difficulty with which you fill in the boxes. If you're struggling to get ideas of inspiration from the Universe to accomplish your thirty-day goal, either you're not connected at a high-enough vibratory level or the goal is not the right one for you at this time, which includes trying to do too much.

For instance, going from being a hundred pounds overweight to sporting a beach body in thirty days isn't possible, no matter how high your vibe is. If the issue is about the right direction at the right time, change your plan up a bit and see if that increases the flow of inspiration. With the weight-loss example, try adjusting your immediate goal to lose ten pounds in thirty days; or in the case of a business start-up, try modifying your launch date to coincide with your publicity plan, rather than rushing to market.

Let's look at another example: Say you want to manifest $100,000 in the next month, but maybe you're not ready to fill in your thirty-day plan because you don't have a clue about where the money will come from. In that case, put your goal aside for a few days, maybe for a week, and turn to creative visualization and high-vibe work. Then come back to your thirty-day plan with your newfound insights, which will increase the flow of ideas, allowing you to fill in all the boxes.

"But I'm Doing What You Said, and It's Not Coming Fast Enough!"

When you put your burning desire out there, *let it go;* when you receive inspiration to move, *take action—*when you're unsure, *raise your energy vibration for answers.* All the while, know deep down that Source Energy is taking care of the rest. If you hang on with a death grip, though, Source Energy won't be able to help you.

Let me give you an example of how this is working in my life right now. I have an unwavering belief—a deep knowing—that the right man is already out there for me and will come into my life when the time is right. I have no doubt about this, not even for a moment. I also have a deep knowing about the reasons he's not here now: (1) I'm still healing my heart and embracing some "me time"; (2) I'm enjoying precious time with my daughter as I watch her grow into a young lady; and (3) I'm aware that the man of my dreams may be going through his own healing right now, and isn't quite ready for me to be a part of his life. I don't have a time schedule for when we'll meet. I just know that we will.

A Final Note

The culmination of your growing fears, hopelessness, and panic can leave you feeling as if you have no control over your life; and the more distractions and chaos you're experiencing, the further you sink. Your way out, though, is through raising your energy vibratory level and keeping it there—do it! Do it often! You will not only change your own life, but you'll help change the face of all humanity at the same time.

You must also be ready and willing to step into the life you want with a deep *knowing* that your new life is waiting for you. Sometimes this requires letting go of some people and things that are not in alignment with what is unfolding for you. Know that your new life is already present and on its way—*feel* that it is already a part of your life . . . and act that way. That's the secret. That's the Holy Grail.

DREAM BIG, my friend!

AFTERWORD

The most important book I've ever read was Napoleon Hill's original edition of *Think and Grow Rich*. It continues to be the key to any success I have enjoyed to date. I have reread passages from *Think and Grow Rich* almost every day since I first discovered the book as a young man.

The book you have just read will likely be the most important book you will ever read, since it brings the essence of Napoleon Hill's wisdom to you in a context that is more aligned with twenty-first century developments. With the addition of the "two Lost Chapters," you will have the full and complete edition, which was not published in the first edition in 1937. We will never know why, for a fact, these two chapters were left out of the original edition, although I have reasoned on numerous occasions that Napoleon Hill's intuition clearly and loudly informed him that the public at large was not ready for such an enormous idea. One of the great mentors I was fortunate enough to have was very emphatic in letting me know that you should never give people an idea larger than they can handle, as it will knock them off balance. Many years later, looking back upon that advice, I'm in full agreement. I believe our intuition is God's way of talking to us. Hill's intuition aptly let him know that the public was not ready for his explanation of the law of vibration.

Today, most everyone is aware that vibration operates on frequencies; our radios, televisions, and telephones operate on frequencies. There are an infinite number of frequencies, and as you study the law of vibration, you will learn that every frequency is hooked up to the one above and the one below. And, if we carry that concept further, we'll start to understand that *every thing* is an expression of the same thing (as above, so below). Science and religion have been teaching us that for a very long time.

Properly understood, the law of vibration will enable you to communicate much more effectively with others. Most professional salespeople have an awareness that if you're going to effectively lead another person to a path of agreement, which is what selling is all about, you must get onto that person's frequency and gently lead them in the direction that you suggest they go. Everything vibrates, whether we are aware of it or not; we live in an ocean of motion.

Riding on the reputation of one of the most recognized authors of the past one-hundred-plus years, Monica Main will be richly rewarded for bringing such important information to the public in such a magnificent manner. As you get to the end of this book, I want you to do what I did almost sixty years ago. When my first mentor gave me my copy of *Think and Grow Rich*, he proposed that Napoleon Hill spent his entire life studying the lives of hundreds of the world's most successful individuals. He then went on to say that he thought it would be a prudent move on my part if I spent the rest of my life attempting to understand what Hill had discovered and shared with the world.

Monica Main has done a wonderful job of adding the "two Lost Chapters" to Hill's masterpiece. I think it would be a prudent move on your part to heed the advice I did many years ago and read Monica's book every day for the rest of your life.

—**Bob Proctor,** the bestselling author of *You Were Born Rich*

FINAL THOUGHTS

I'm sitting in Tuscany, Italy, listening to the unusual chirping of some exotic-looking birds while gazing over a beautiful, never-ending vineyard that touches a sun-setting horizon. I see a crumbling home off in the distance and wonder if part of it was touched by the Germans during World War II. It reminds me of how much history there is here, and all the while there's a sense of innocence that is revealed in the Italians' food, the plants they grow, their wines, and their little towns that canvas the country. I love Italy and its people. This space helps me feel centered, satisfied, and blissful.

What's significant about this trip is that I brought my dad along. I hadn't seen him in two years, but I've learned to forgive and forget, which has given me more peace and personal power than ever. I realize that all of life—good, bad, and otherwise—is absolutely perfect, always has been, and always will be. The things that have happened, and will happen, are all part of the Divine Order of the Universe. I feel a sense of bliss . . . I just can't describe how life changing it is and how awesome it is to feel this way. *Try it.* You may become addicted to feeling amazing, just as I have.

I'm so honored to have been able to bring you the Lost Chapters of Napoleon Hill's *Think and Grow Rich.* And I'm particularly excited about the magical new future that is *at your command* once you begin implementing the secrets within this book. I just know that you're embarking on a magical journey!

May you finally *allow* Source Energy to be a big part of your life . . . now and forevermore.

—**Monica Main**

ABOUT NAPOLEON HILL

Born Oliver Napoleon Hill in a one-room cabin in Pound, Virginia, on October 26, 1883, Hill was always something of a forward thinker, and well ahead of his time. His ideas on success combined with metaphysical components took the world by storm with the book *Think and Grow Rich*, published in 1937, and has since sold more than a hundred million copies worldwide, making it one of the most successful books of all time.

Hill experienced both ups and downs when it came to his own personal fortunes. He had been criticized for his ability to write about wealth but his inability to consistently generate it for himself through his own business and investment activities. During his time, the only things he could claim as success, really, were his books about wealth. What most didn't understand, however, is that Napoleon Hill did accomplish his *burning desire* to be a successful writer. He had little interest in having a business or investments of his own.

He saw his life's purpose to be to open the hearts and minds of the common man and woman by unveiling the secrets of the Universe, to help each and every one of us understand that we have the innate ability to create whatever we want out of ourselves— wealth or something else. He was truly one of the original pioneers of the New Thought Movement. Napoleon Hill has taught us that even the meekest can become the grandest.

ABOUT MONICA MAIN

Monica Main is a successful entrepreneur and self-made millionaire who has used unconventional wealth-attraction techniques to best leverage her massive success. Having grown up in the Chicago suburbs in the '70s and '80s, adhering to the spiritual philosophy of Kriya Yoga, a Hindu-based form of wisdom taught by Paramahansa Yogananda starting in 1920, Main was able to masterfully blend these teachings with those of forward thinkers such as Charles Haanel, Napoleon Hill, Joseph Campbell, Louise Hay, and Dr. Wayne Dyer, to name just a few.

In 1987, Monica discovered a powerful technique that combined visualization with vibrational quantum physics, which changed her entire life. However, as she entered her teenage years, her secret of manifestation was swept under the carpet as the heaviness of some major life changes took hold. Having clawed her way to the top in her career and business field even though she'd gone through three divorces, a short stint in federal prison due to an unfortunate business mistake, a personal bankruptcy, and a devastating two-year civil lawsuit with the government, she found herself completely tapped out psychologically, mentally, emotionally, and spiritually. Even still, she was always able to land on her feet with continued business success but always felt as if something was missing in her life. Since discovering the two Lost Chapters of Napoleon Hill's *Think and Grow Rich* in 2017, Main's entire life took a 180-degree turn in the most glorious, blissful, and prosperous ways imaginable—in both her personal and business worlds, and she's now ready to bring these secrets to you.

Website: **www.MonicaMain.com**